Additional Stories
from My Journey

Ed Hearn

Additional Stories from My Journey

Staying the Course

LEGACY IV BOOKS

Published by Legacy IV Books

ehearn1234@gmail.com

Published 2024

Copyright © 2024 by Ed Hearn

ISBN 9798345235058

Printed in the United States of America

Set in Times New Roman

Editing and proofreading by Trent Armbruster and Gail Hearn

Design by Abigail Chiaramonte

Cover photo by David Straight

Dedication

I'd like to say, "thank you" and dedicate this sixth memoir book, in the continuing 'My Journey' series of short stories, to my loving sister Gail Alyne Hearn, who has helped me immensely throughout the entire writing process with non-stop encouragement, editing advice, and proofreading skills. She deserves a great deal of credit for having supported me in everything I've attempted and accomplished throughout life.

Preface

During my preparation and before writing this sixth book in a growing series, I began to think about how each individual story in my preceding five memoir books had actually affected me. With each one, I was mentally transported back in time and given the opportunity to relive different moments from my life, a few of which I'd almost forgotten ever occurred. Those journeys were all good and together offered me an overview of who I was and who I'd become. They collectively gave me the chance to evaluate a progression of events which caused my life to slowly evolve all the way from being a young kid growing up in a financially stressed family, to a hard-working individual in mid-life with seemingly non-stop responsibilities, to a wiser and older retired person in his mid-seventies.

What I can honestly say, with little hesitation, is that life has been a wild ride. But…I think I'd do it all again, the same way as the first time, if I had the chance. That's probably a normal response when looking backward for most of us, while staying focused on many of the positive things which took place in prior years.

For me, there's been continuous wide swings back and forth between emotional highs and lows. I guess everyone has gone through similar experiences where they've only been allowed short periods of time to catch their breath before circumstances change once again. My highs, or extremely good times, were usually followed by moderate, or deep lows. Sometimes, those lows seemed to go on for years, but eventually they faded, and I'd once again find myself back in good spirits and on top of the world in a better place. Because of having experienced some of those unavoidable life events, I'm a firm believer that in order to fully appreciate the good times, it's first necessary to experience some of the really tough times which invariably come along. Recognizing a contrast between the two extremes is what's important. By doing so, I've been able to gain a greater appreciation for life in general and realize everything will eventually get better as a result of my staying focused on the positive side of things.

The varying ways in which our successes and failures affect us throughout life are part of a cycle and fall into a unique category of ups and downs. Hopefully we've all enjoyed periods of time where we've felt successful, and things were going well. But... for some people, those times are few and far between. That's truly sad. Being able to experience small successes usually leads to large successes, just as thinking positively can lead to a person who is happy and pleased with themselves.

In writing my memoir stories, I've tried as much as possible to share the high points which occurred in my life by keeping most everything upbeat. Occasionally, I've written about a few dark times, but those were purposely kept to a minimum. There's a reason for that handling. During my thirty years of working as an outside salesperson and regularly dealing with customers one-on-one, I learned they really didn't want to hear details about unpleasant things which might have been taking place in my personal life. If I didn't have something positive to say about myself, I'd usually re-direct the conversation so they could talk about themselves. That approach proved to be an important golden touch, when accompanied by a wide smile. As a result, it usually led to me being given a nice order where I could make a small commission for my efforts.

What you'll find within this sixth book is a collection of short stories which individually hold varying tidbits of value. Each one of them meant something special to me. Some are true tales from my past and some are thoughtful reflections being brought forth from an aging and mature mind. Those latter ones I just mentioned are the stories I probably like the best.

After finishing the last story in this book, and those coming before it, maybe you'll recognize a similarity between your life and mine. We're all on a journey together. Sometimes that journey is unique, but many times it contains elements which are very familiar to all of us.

In conclusion, I want to encourage you, the reader, to write your own memoir. There's no time better than today to get started. To leave your life's legacy in the form of short stories would be the best gift you could possibly offer your children, grandchildren, and many others who might benefit. When the book gets published, you'll be able to hold a finished copy in your hand and present it to others with great pride. I'm aware of that fact from firsthand experience and highly recommend it to each and every one of you.

Contents

The Old Letter

You know…sometimes it's okay to be sentimental. I'm making that statement based on my discovery of a long-lost treasure, which was just uncovered this morning. I was in the process of moving a group of large cardboard boxes from my garage to an upstairs storage room, following our recent move into a new home, and ran across a collection of old photographs that had been mounted in an album over thirty years ago. There'd been times I'd spent a great deal of effort trying to find that particular item, only to finally give up, with the thought it somehow must have been discarded by accident.

Approximately one hundred color photos had been carefully placed in clear, vinyl pockets with four to a sheet. The album's cover was a heavy, dark blue leather with gold-stamped accents. As I held it in my hands, I could hardly believe it still existed. One photo after the other, which my younger sister had long ago inserted into the album, showed the step-by-step construction of a home I'd had built between January 1991 and December of 1992.

After we moved in, I received the album from her as a surprise gift and was thrilled to get it. I knew she'd regularly gone by the construction site with my dad and had taken those progressive photographs with her camera, so she could present them to me at a future date. While turning the pages and carefully studying each image, I was reminded of all the work I'd done to plan and oversee that project as the days and weeks slowly progressed. When it was all complete, I was extremely proud of the structure I knew would serve our entire family for years to come.

Shown in many of the photographs was my dad. He was obviously excited for me with what was taking place, and it showed on his face by his wide smile as he looked into the camera's lens.

I knew that without my dad having laid the groundwork with his lifelong struggle to support our family, I would not have been able to go to college, get a good job, and ultimately afford to build that house. It was bigger and nicer than what he and my mom lived in after forty years of him working a boring, blue-collar job at a local factory.

As I flipped from one page of photos to another, a folded sheet of notebook paper fell out. I instantly knew it must contain something important, or it wouldn't have been stuck in there. After opening it, a date jumped out at me that had been written at the very top. It was February 23, 1994. That date had a great deal of significance because it was quickly identified as my dad's birthday. In 1994, on that date, he would have been seventy-three years old.

I began to read the letter with a heightened degree of interest. It was instantly recognized as something I'd written shortly after we'd moved into that new house and was the first draft of what I'd later copied to a birthday card I sent him.

Here's what it said:

2/23/94

Happy Birthday, Dad! I cannot decide what to get you, so I decided to share some of my personal feelings instead. Maybe my thoughts are more important than physical objects. In looking back over the years of our lives together, always with fond memories, how I feel now can be best stated by what my nine-year-old son, Matt, recently said to me. I asked him why he loved me, and his reply was, "Because you do things with me, and you take time to include me when you go places." I felt those were important points.

I can remember the many fishing trips you and I made together, a number of eventful camping outings, and our family vacations. I can remember the many times you came to my high school athletic events, including numerous football games, late night basketball games, and track events. I remember the long trips you made to be present for some of my sporting events while I was in college, when the distance was not convenient, and how supportive you've always been of everything I've attempted.

You have always been willing to help me with any project I came up with, when I needed your participation. That has meant even more to me lately, as I've realized how tired I am after a full day's work at the office and the kids ask me to do something with them at home.

Most of all, I admire your ability to 'hang in there.' Stability in a relationship is something I don't see much in our society. Your example of staying with your marriage and family is probably the reason I have now made it twenty-four years with the same wife, and I'm able to enjoy my two wonderful boys, in spite of some serious marital issues we've had.

I must say, on your birthday, "Thanks" for what you've given me. I love you very much and wish you many more years of health and happiness.

Your son,

Ed

As it turned out, my dad only had one more birthday to celebrate. He died in the fall of 1995 of congestive heart failure. Looking back on those photos from roughly thirty years ago, they bring back a variety of memories. Most all of them are good ones. If I could turn back the clock, I'd give my dad a big hug and tell him one more time, "Dad, I love you."

Some of what I learned about living... and dying...from Mr. Bradley

Back in the early spring of 2002, a little puppy born in Minneapolis, Minnesota was destined to have a huge impact on my life. Starting more than a year earlier, I'd located on the Internet a lady in that city by the name of Margaret Seaman, who was a breeder of a unique line of American cocker spaniels. She'd spent twenty years of selective breeding to obtain a special coloring for her bloodline. Instead of the black, white, and maybe a little tan coloring usually seen on a parti-colored American cocker, she'd focused on developing one with the more predominate colors of a springer spaniel, which sported deep brown patches over a base of white.

Shortly after viewing photos of her newest litter containing beautiful, cute puppies shown online, I decided to purchase one of her dogs in the near future. My first phone call to Margaret ended in disappointment, in that I requested to buy 'the pick of the litter' from one of her future breedings between two of her highly regarded AKC champion dogs. I was told that the same request had already been made for the next scheduled breeding by another individual, carrying my wishes forward into the following year. At that time, I also stated my plans to show the puppy in dog shows around the country and somewhere down the road breed it, so the puppies could be sold. She was okay knowing I was planning to show the dog but hesitated with my request to breed it. She wanted to retain all rights to future reproduction, backed up by a signed contract between us, or I had to agree to have the dog neutered. That was not part of my plans.

During three additional phone calls over the next year, I repeatedly asked her to sell me one of her pups and allow me to select my choice for showing and later breeding. Finally, she gave in. I was told a new litter would be born during the middle of March in 2002, and I would be given the first choice. Because of my sustained interest, she had concluded that I'd be a responsible and loving owner.

At the age of nine weeks, Mr. Bradley arrived on a jet plane from Minnesota in his own little travel cage. We picked him up in Raleigh, North Carolina two hours from our home in Wilmington, and were thrilled to see him for the first time. He arrived alone and had been placed in the baggage compartment of the plane. Over the next few weeks, I spent many hours regularly taking him outside for intense house training. Bradley became the focus of my attention, and we bonded as a result.

At the age of ten months, he was entered into his first local dog show where he won Best of Variety. That successful beginning led to us hiring a professional trainer from Knoxville, Tennessee who took him around the country to various shows throughout the fall of 2002 and into the spring of 2003.

Before we knew it, he'd earned thirty-eight ribbons in various shows and became a full-fledged American Kennel Club Champion after traveling to many different states, including Montana, Mississippi, and Louisiana.

Once he attained the prestigious title of champion, he simply returned home to settle in as a member of our family. Most every day throughout his life, which extended to sixteen and a half years, I regularly walked outside spending endless hours with him in the morning and later in the afternoon. Even though I'd originally planned to breed him and make money from the sale of his puppies, that never occurred. He just became our valued house companion and was treated like a king. That's how he eventually was given the official name of Mr. Bradley. His registered AKC show name was Tri Beau Bradley. He was a tri-color cocker with a base of solid white fur, major patches of chocolate brown, and touches of light tan in select areas. He was a beautiful little guy, only fifteen inches in height at the shoulders.

Many days Mr. Bradley would quietly sit in my lap while

I watched television. I'd look down at him as he'd stare up at me with his alert, brown eyes and wonder what was running through his mind. There was no doubt that a high degree of intelligence controlled his actions based on how he reacted to stimuli throughout each day. It got to the point where I knew he understood exactly what I said to him. At other times, I innately knew what he wanted from me. We communicated effectively, even though he couldn't talk.

By nature, his strong personality pushed for him to be in control as much as I'd allow. For instance, when we went walking, he determined what direction we were to travel, how long he wanted to stay in one place, and when he was ready to return home. I'd let him have his way and felt good about doing that for him. The way I looked at it, he was confined to the inside of our house most of the time, so my feelings were that he deserved a degree of real freedom to make a few of his own decisions whenever possible.

My emotional connection with Mr. Bradley increased as each year passed. Whenever we happened to be out of town on vacation and he stayed with a friend, I'd worry about how he might be coping without us. The little guy was always glad to see us upon our return and wasted no time in letting us know he'd had a good time. He never held a grudge, never acted offended, and clearly understood that we loved him.

I began to consider the contrast between his way of being and the way people in general react to situations. In my opinion, people seem to be much more emotional and unpredictable. Because of that, sometimes it's hard to know where you stand with them. But...with Mr. Bradley, every day was a new one, and he'd quickly return the love he was given. If anything happened between us, which I might feel bad about, I knew he'd soon forgive me and move forward. We were always best buddies...no matter what. He was a worthy and trusted companion. Occasionally, while walking with him, I'd think about how different it would be if we could say the same thing about all our friends throughout life.

Over the years, as he aged, I observed Mr. Bradley work through numerous health issues. After turning nine, he suddenly developed glaucoma in his right eye. The eyeball began to swell, and we were told by an eye specialist that he'd already gone blind in that eye, and it needed to be removed due to excess internal pressure. The surgery was performed and surprisingly he came out of it acting as if he was just fine. The observable, living eye tissue had been saved, and internally a small silicone ball was inserted to replace the normal liquid inside. Since his eyes were dark brown, it wasn't obvious he'd lost sight in that eye. We knew he couldn't see out of it, but that didn't seem to bother him. He just adjusted.

A few years later, the veterinarian noticed an inflammation in his lower front gums and determined he had cancer across the front part of his lower mouth. As a result, the entire front part of his inner and lower jaw was removed, along with several teeth, leaving only his back molders to chew food against a normal top layer of teeth. The surgeon was so skillful that even without that section of bone and teeth in his mouth, it wasn't very noticeable what had taken place. To eat food, he'd gum it into his mouth and chew in the back area before swallowing. Again, he just adjusted to the situation and went on with his life.

Upon approaching his sixteenth birthday, Mr. Bradley began to finally show signs of old age. It was clear he couldn't hear as well as in the past. He'd become occasionally disoriented and ultimately began to have trouble walking on our slick wood floors without falling. His leg muscles became so weak that his legs would slip out from under him while walking. We purchased a few, long, rug runners to help him grip the surface and that made his walking inside the house easier.

I was committed to helping him survive as long as possible. One day I sat down with him and looked into his face and quietly said, "Old man, I'm in no hurry to lose you as my companion. You've been way too good for me over a long period of time. I'll do everything I can, if you try to hang in there. When you're finally ready to go…let me know. Until that time, I've got your back."

I instinctively knew he understood. From that time on, and for the following six months, I worked with him day and night to constantly provide for his needs. He arrived at the time where he couldn't hold his bowels past a point, so I'd get up multiple times throughout the night and we'd go walking around the neighborhood so he could do his business. Those trips during the night, which interrupted my sleep, kept me completely exhausted during the daytime, but I felt I owed him my heartfelt efforts.

Finally, the time arrived. He was in bad shape. The vet was asked to come to our home and put him to sleep. For the three hours before his death, he and I visited the same places around the neighborhood we'd been to hundreds of times together. We quietly walked together as I was aware that within hours he would be gone. Somehow, I think he knew it was time to go.

After it was all over, I cried like a baby. I'd lost my close friend of many years.

In the end, I realized he'd taught me how to die gracefully. Without complaint, he moved on to another place.

From Mr. Bradley, I learned a lot about living and also a lot about dying. I miss the little guy and all he meant to me. He was one of life's true treasures.

The Christmas Card

A dark red, oversized envelope had been mailed from Mansfield, Texas and later arrived in my mailbox on a Friday, during the middle part of December. The year was 2021. I could hardly believe the person's name which was shown in block lettering on its upper left corner. As I stared at the handwritten, black ink, a chill ran down my spine. Could it be that a dear old friend had somehow found me in this big old world after fifty years?

Without hesitation, I ripped open the side flap and removed a Christmas card. Tiny specks of silver glitter accentuated its front illustration. There was a colorful drawing showing a winter scene with a country home in a wooded area and a snowman in the yard. To the bottom right of the card, there was a pre-printed message which read, 'The special people we care about are always close in thought.' At that moment, I didn't know what to think or say.

Inside, there was wording which was simple and direct. It said, "Merry Christmas…your friend, Roy." I knew which 'Roy' was being referred to because of the name I'd seen, that was shown as part of the return address, on the envelope's front. There was also a short bit of additional information on the inside of the card, including his telephone number.

The last time I'd seen or heard from Roy was in May of 1971. After graduating that month, I returned to my hometown in central Tennessee, and I felt sure he moved to his hometown in southern Florida after his own graduation the following year. He was one year behind me with his studies.

We'd been teammates on the college track and field team for

three years, where both of us regularly trained together through-out the week. Full athletic scholarships had been awarded to each of us that enabled us to live in the same dorm which housed all the school's athletes. We usually ate for free at the school's cafeteria after our workouts and naturally enjoyed a lot of the same friends. The best way to put it is that Roy and I were good buddies.

Every year, we competed alongside each other throughout the spring outdoor season, as we both threw the shot put and discus while representing our school in those events. He was able to outdistance me in both of those activities, but I also competed in the javelin event, where I excelled. The javelin throw became my specialty. There weren't many who could outdistance me in that event across the entire country during that timeframe.

Roy had to be one of the strongest individuals I'd ever met. He could easily bench press close to four hundred pounds and squat with an arched barbell across his broad shoulders hold-ing up to five hundred pounds. One time he and another ath-lete placed that heavier barbell, loaded to the maximum, on my shoulders as I stood between two support poles, so I could expe-rience the weight. Within seconds, my legs began to shake and quiver. I begged for it to be removed before I collapsed, which almost occurred.

The reason I remember the last time I saw Roy was the fact that during the latter part of May in 1971, we traveled together to Wichita, Kansas to compete in the United States National Track and Field Championships. Our measured distances and perfor-mances for the entire spring season in our two different events had qualified us for that prestigious competition. On that occa-sion, Roy participated in the shot put event, while I competed in the javelin event. The trip marked the end of my college eligibil-ity, while he still had one more year to go.

While waiting to leave our college campus in east Tennessee for the long drive west to Kansas with our coach, Roy and I stood in the foyer of a large building designated as the Student Union. Without saying a word, he turned and walked over to a black piano that was positioned in the center of its main room. Some of the most beautiful music I'd ever heard began to flow out of that instrument as Roy's fingers moved effortlessly across the keyboard. He could have been in Carnegie Hall playing before a large crowd of admirers with classical music by Mozart and Beethoven, but I was the only observer.

Stunned by what I was hearing, I approached him and asked, "When did you learn to play like that? I've known you and been around you daily for the past three years and you never told me you could play the piano."

"To tell you the truth, Ed, I was a little embarrassed to let anyone know I could play. As a kid, my mom pushed me to take lessons for twelve years while growing up. Since you're about to leave school following this trip, I thought you might want to see something else I can do other than sports."

My mouth just hung open. I said, "I'm shocked. What you're capable of doing is unbelievable. You should have told me much earlier about this skill. I greatly admire your ability and the music is incredible. Thanks for showing me this other side of yourself."

"Glad to do it," was all he humbly said in reply.

Within five minutes, our coach pulled up out front. We crawled into his car and off we went to Kansas.

Shortly after that trip was completed, I never saw Roy again.

While still staring at the Christmas card and reflecting on all of those distant memories which had just moved through my mind, I picked up the phone and dialed the number he'd written inside the card. Roy answered on the third ring with the same old familiar voice I'd heard so many times in the past.

"I said, "Just got your card. How did you get my address? How in the hell are you doing?"

"I'm fine, but much older than when we were last together.

Moved to Texas a few years ago. Can you believe how long it's been since we were in college? Found your address on the Internet and thought I'd mail you a card. I guess it was a big surprise to hear from me after all these years?"

"You've got that right. It's been fifty years. Am I correct?"

"Yep…a long time."

Our conversation went on for about thirty minutes with one question after another being asked in rapid fire about what we'd done with our lives. That included things such as, 'Where did your career carry you?' 'Who did you marry?' 'How many kids do you have?' On and on it went. I was extremely interested, and I'm sure he was also.

Finally, it was time to hang up. Before doing so, I recommended that we make plans to get together in the future. He was all for it and said he wanted to introduce me to his new girlfriend in that he was divorced. I wanted to do the same.

Just as the call was about to end, I asked, "Back when we were in college, you once showed me a photo of two twin girls who were about two years old, and you told me they were your daughters. After that day, you never mentioned them again. How in the world are they doing?"

"Ed, thanks for asking. The girls have been a blessing to me. They're both in their early fifties. As you know, both you and I are now roughly seventy-two. They're my only children, and I love them very much. How many kids do you have?"

"I've got two boys. One is forty-three and the other is thirty-seven. Great kids. I've also got two grandchildren, a girl and a boy, ages twelve and ten. Both are growing like weeds. Before I hang up, I want to thank you for looking up my address and sending me the Christmas card. To hear from you again is fantastic. I'm sure you remember what your card had to say on the front which was very meaningful and instantly grabbed my attention. It read, 'The special people we care about are always close in thought.' I want you to know that I've often thought about the years we spent together so long ago, but I didn't know there was a way to locate you. Now, that connection has been made. Let's stay in touch."

"You bet, my friend. You take care."

"I will, and you do the same."

Memorable Moments in Sports

During my high school and college days of track and field competition, most everyone was aware of the world record that had been set by Roger Bannister in the mile run. He'd broken the "four-minute barrier" on May 6, 1954, by finishing with an unbelievable time of 3 minutes, 59.4 seconds. He was twenty-five years old at the time. Before that occurred, many thought to run that fast for an entire mile was humanly impossible.

On June 9th, 2023, a Norwegian distance runner named Jakob Ingebrigtsen shattered the old world record for two miles by running that event in 7 minutes, 54.10 seconds at the Paris Diamond League Championship. He was only 22 years of age. His recent finish is viewed as an even greater accomplishment than what Roger Bannister achieved in 1954 because of the outstanding pace he was able to sustain for twice the distance.

The previous world record for the two-mile race was held by Kenya's Daniel Komen with a time of 7 minutes, 58.61 seconds, and was set on July 19, 1997. He held that record for approximately 25 years. He's the only other man in history to officially run the two-mile race in under 8 minutes.

For someone such as myself, those accomplishments are overwhelming, and something I can hardly believe. They bring to mind a time when I was quite young and just getting started in athletics.

Back in the year of 1962, I was in the eighth grade, short, and a little on the chubby side. Our high school track coach, who was always recruiting for the team by getting younger kids started early, approached me one day and asked, "Would you be interested in being part of our school's track team and run the mile at all of our competitions?"

I didn't know how to respond. How could he think I would be able to come anywhere close to finishing in a respectable position along with the more mature athletes we already had participating in that event who were juniors and seniors?

Being taken by surprise with his question, I responded, "If you believe I can run the mile as part of the team and not completely embarrass the school in the process, I'll give it a go."

"Fine," he replied. "I'll see you at the track this afternoon after classes are over for the day. I realize this may be a little early to get you started with athletics, but I see you as someone I can train over the next few years while you develop physically. You'll have a good time. I'll also be recruiting some of your other friends that are about your same age, so you won't be in this by yourself."

At three o'clock that afternoon, I was dressed in official running shorts and a tee shirt, wearing my high top, Converse tennis shoes.

The coach approached me and said, "I'm glad you're here. You and three other boys from your class will be working together. The other three are already jogging around the track. That's what I want you to do. Get the feel for our cinder track and learn to enjoy the crunch under your shoes. Before long, you'll look forward to being here each afternoon with your friends. For today, why don't you plan to jog around our quarter mile track four times. That'll be a full mile."

"Okay, coach. I'll give it my best."

That day, I learned the actual length of a mile and was totally exhausted after four laps. Each day afterwards, I showed up and repeated my efforts, slowly picking up speed over the next few weeks. Eventually, I found myself able to run even farther on every outing, as my body adjusted to the intense exercise. In the process, I actually lost a few pounds and began to feel better about myself.

It wasn't long before the school's first official track meet was to take place. Because most of the student body tended to show up for our athletic events, I expected there to be around 700 fans in the stands cheering for our team. My nerves were on edge when the mile run was announced to begin in only a few minutes. Looking into the crowd, I noticed some of my classmates smiling broadly and staring directly at me.

The starting gun was soon raised, it fired a single shot causing a loud noise, and we were off and running. I knew from practice sessions that I needed to pace myself in order to be able to finish four laps around the track, so my first lap was slower than the rest. With each lap, I picked up additional speed.

Somewhere near the end of my third quarter of a mile, I was lapped by two other runners. Both were seniors and one of them was a member of our team who had some of the best times in the city that year. I watched from across the oval field as they soon sprinted down the straightaway toward the finish line, while I still had almost three-fourths of a lap to complete. Glancing behind me, I noticed I was in last place. That was fine, because I'd set my goal at the beginning of the race to be sure to finish and do that with as little embarrassment as possible.

As I rounded the last curve and began to run down the final 100 yards, the crowd began to cheer louder than before. The grandstands were suddenly full of standing individuals clapping and making a lot of noise. I could hardly believe it. Adrenalin pumped through my body, so I picked up speed. Finally, it was over. I'd run my first mile in competition and was proud of the accomplishment.

The coach walked over and put his arm around my shoulders. "Good job, Eddie. Even though you finished last, you gave it everything you had. I'm happy for you."

All I could say in response was, "Thanks, coach. I'll do better next time."

With that introduction to the world of organized sports in the eighth grade, it later encouraged me to participate in four years of high school track, four years of basketball, and four years of football.

Many years later, after graduating from college, where I attended all four years on a track scholarship, I saw that coach at a high school reunion sitting on the far side of the room. I walked over and shook his hand.

I said, "I want to say, 'thank you,' for your efforts so long ago in including me on your track team. That first year, while I was still in the eighth grade and ran the mile as part of your team, started my lifelong love for sports and a personal involvement in those activities. Back then, I learned exactly how far it was to complete an entire mile, and what it was like to push your body to the limit. That experience has served me well over the years. It gave me an appreciation for other athletes who train hard and compete successfully that I wouldn't have known fully without your help and encouragement. Thank you, again."

He looked me in the eyes and said, "All I did was to get you started. You did the rest. It was my job as the coach to encourage everyone and help them reach their full potential. Thanks for coming to me now and expressing your gratitude."

I left that gathering with an appreciative heart. On my way to the car, memories poured through my mind of past events, and a true gentleman who'd taken his time to encourage and help untold numbers of kids over his long career in an effort to get them started on the right path in life. I knew I was a better person because of his association with me.

I miss that man, and I miss those times so long ago when I participated in the mile run for my school, while attending the eighth grade.

A Lesson in Humility

Just a few days ago an unusual happening took me by complete surprise. It occurred during a buffet lunch at one of my favorite places where I normally relax and enjoy a heaping plate of good old southern cooking.

After arriving and going through a long line to pay for my upcoming meal, I noticed an available seat located near the back of the main room. Looking around, the restaurant was full of men and women, all busy filling their plates or already seated in small groups engaged in conversation.

Just as all the others had done, I picked up a clean plate from a stack on a nearby table, walked over to a series of stainless-steel countertops containing rows of various food items, and began to fill it. Waiting on myself was normal, and I knew the routine. Before long, I had mounded large helpings of assorted vegetables on my plate, along with a generous serving of fried chicken. My mouth began to water after I glanced down at the selections I'd made. There was no doubt I was hungry.

A waitress I'd known for many years stopped by and asked, "Is there anything else you need?"

Without hesitation, I replied, "Nope...I believe I'm in good shape for the moment."

Being friendly and engaging in a quick bit of conversation, she asked another question, "Anything new happening this week?"

"Well...interesting that you ask. Today's my birthday."

"Well...Happy birthday to you."

"Thanks," I said.

When she walked away without asking how old I was, I sat motionless for a moment and thought, *either she really doesn't care or doesn't want to embarrass me with that direct question.*

It didn't take long for the situation to change. A much older man sitting only one table away had overheard her question, followed by my response, before leaning forward toward me.

In almost a whisper, he said, "You've got my curiosity up because just last week I also had a birthday. If you'll tell me your current age, I'll tell you mine."

I thought to myself, *this guy looks quite old and has got to be close to ninety, so I'll have some fun and exaggerate my age to see what he says.*

Before I could stop myself, a boldfaced lie left my lips. I figured there was no way he would believe me. The response I made was, "Today's my eightieth birthday."

Without even blinking an eye or questioning my statement in any way, he responded, "Got ya by three years."

Actually, I had just turned seventy-four. I had been positive he'd know I was nowhere near eighty and get a good laugh.

His response meant he was eighty-three. From his body language and lack of questioning, he apparently felt confident I was eighty.

I was stunned. *Do I really look that old?* ran through my mind.

Without any hesitation, I felt compelled to immediately straighten out my failed attempt at humor. I said, "I apologize, sir. I was just kidding. I'm actually seventy-four, as of today, and not eighty. I thought you'd pick up on my white lie, so we could together have a good laugh. I guess I'm looking older than I thought."

"Ah…don't worry about it. We all play those little games with others as we get older. Even though I didn't say anything, I knew you weren't eighty or anywhere close to it. I was just playing along with ya. Seventy-four's a good age. Enjoy it. When you get to be my age, you'll look back and consider yourself, as you are now, a young man."

"Thanks…I needed that."

"No problem. Let's eat what we've got on our plates and then get up and get a refill of this good food."

"I'll be right behind ya."

Dance while you're able.
Laugh when you get a chance.
Use time as if it matters.
Enjoy life as you advance.

The moments move swiftly.
There's much to achieve.
It's all a wonderful adventure,
for those who truly believe.

Ed Hearn

Perseverance

"If at first you don't succeed…try, try again." We've all heard that familiar battle cry.

I'll be one to openly admit, that's what I've spent my entire life doing. What I'm implying by that original statement has to do with the latter half, the 'try, try again' part. There's been many different activities in which I've attempted to achieve a high degree of success over the years, only to realize there was much more work involved than could have ever been comprehended. For some unknown reason, that never seemed to hold me back. Inside, there was a determined motivation, focused in only one direction. That direction was to ultimately achieve success at all costs. The need to succeed was always stronger than my willingness to give up.

Somehow, I realized early on that focus and persistence were necessary ingredients.

During high school days in the 60s, my goal was to achieve some of the best grades possible in every subject. That caused me to spend extra time in the late evening hours reading and studying hard to stay ahead of the pack. All of that work resulted in being awarded the honor of Valedictorian upon graduation. Along with that title, I ended my four years of high school with the highest grade-point-average of anyone who'd ever attended the school.

Shortly after regular classes were over in the afternoon, I always stayed busy for an average of two to three hours each day being an active participant in one of our organized team sports, which included football, track and field, and basketball, depending on the time of year.

Becoming part of our varsity basketball squad in the eighth grade, originally as a member of the 'B' team, challenged me to stay aggressive, so I could eventually move up to occupy a key spot on the 'A' team. That occurred faster than I thought possible. For the following two years, I dressed out for all the premier games and regularly played in front of a gym full of people for at least a portion of each outing. My junior and senior years were spent as a full-time player who was one of the main five on the court for the entire game.

College worked to be a similar experience with me putting out a tremendous amount of extra effort to achieve a better-than-normal outcome in athletics. Even though I wasn't given a scholarship after high school, early within the first year as a freshman, I earned the respect of my track and field coach to the extent he awarded me a full, four-year athletic scholarship to throw the shot put, discus, and javelin.

By the end of my senior year, I'd set the all-time school record and won the entire conference championship in the javelin event. That distance record set in competition has never been broken and is still recognized as the best in the school's history.

Even though it's been said I have a type 'A' personality and I'm an overachiever, I don't think that's entirely accurate for me. I've just always had a strong desire to be the best I can be…at everything in which I've taken a strong interest. It's mostly an inner thing. I figure I'm only going to go around once in this life, so why not go 'all in.'

Over my lifetime, when I've wanted to master something specific, I knew it would take a super amount of effort and focus which few people would be willing to give. That's where perseverance and the familiar saying comes in…the, 'try, try again' part of life. Success is usually gained through repeated effort, study, and practice…to the extreme. No one achieves great success without exceptional effort.

The business world works about the same way. Unless an

individual has been able to inherit wealth that someone else earned by their hard work, countless hours must be spent just 'grinding it out.' It helps tremendously to be intelligent and get a few breaks here and there, but overall, success comes down to good-old hard work and the positive attitude of never giving up.

I was able to make a huge success out of my thirty-year career in business and retired at the young age of fifty. The last twenty-five years have been icing-on-the-cake, as they say. For a hobby, I've been creating top-notch bronze sculptures for many years and enjoy showing them to friends, along with selling a few.

Life seems to reward those who treat it with respect. By that, I mean 'those who learn early on what's required.' There's no entitlement to be gained, no free lunch...or at least there wasn't for me.

I'm glad I was able to personally taste true success more than one time throughout my long life. Let me say, I've found, "Success is much better than failure." If there's one thing I can offer, it's my heartfelt encouragement for anyone desiring that same outcome, to pick something in life that is meaningful to them and give it everything they've got to make it a success. But...always remember, "It's not so much about the destination, as it is about the journey. The journey is where all the action and fun takes place."

The Joy of Writing

How much better can it get than to be able to look back over your life, after you've passed the age of seventy, and have the opportunity to write about some of your past experiences? I find it one of the true 'joys of living.' In my opinion, it's important to understand what has taken place and why.

Since my early retirement from the business world, when there was suddenly a great deal of free time to do whatever I wanted, I've taken the time to include special moments to sit at my computer and just write. Because I only feel the need to please myself, that creativity seems to take about any direction it needs to go. The realization is always there that I really don't have to share it with anyone else, if I choose. With that knowledge, it completely frees me and never allows 'writer's block syndrome' to get in the way. Many writers feel pressured to end up with a literary masterpiece every time they begin to compose something new. There's none of that for me.

Many times, I just write about whatever seems to be on my mind at a particular time and thereby end with short essays, which I call 'memoir stories.' It's not uncommon for those to surprise me, since the words just seem to flow onto paper, as if they're not really coming from me. I find it amazing what my inner consciousness can generate if allowed to operate with no restriction.

Everyone has followed a different course through their strange journey called 'life,' to get to the place they now find themselves. But...not everyone wants to remember all the details of how they got there. In my case, I want to know how and why I'm now where I am. What decisions along the way got me to this current state of mind and physical destination? In order to work all of that out in my mind and arrive at a place of peace, I must evaluate the details. At my current age, there's plenty of those to consider.

As I move forward through each day, I find myself frequently taking time to reflect on various past events which directed my life in one way or the other. I can now see more clearly how even small decisions caused my life to change and evolve, sometimes for the good and sometimes for the bad. As they say, "Hindsight is twenty-twenty." That old phrase, I believe, means that once everything's all said and done, a person can go back in their mind, take a look at the facts, and view the past with a lot more clarity.

By taking the time to write on paper some of my memories, going all the way back to my youth, it's been possible to sort through how I eventually arrived at this present moment. When I talk to a few people, it's not uncommon for them to tell me, "I really don't want to bring up the past again. Those memories bring back so much which was very hard on me emotionally and physically, that I'd rather just forget about it."

At the same time, many other individuals are quite interested in talking about what they've been through and have an inner need to reflect on those happenings. Those are the ones I try and encourage to sit down and write a few simple stories about themselves. I know that by doing so, they'll become more aware of how their lives have progressed, why they made different decisions, and be able to see the results of their efforts. In a sense, they'll become more appreciative of what's been accomplished.

Writing can serve the purpose of allowing the mind to release emotions that would otherwise cause stress and worry. By putting thoughts on paper, it's liberating. At the same time, there's a feeling which develops that the time spent will provide something of real value as an end result. It's a win-win proposition.

I think everyone should, somewhere during their lifetime, sit down and write a series of short stories about themselves and the way they view the world. That cannot be accomplished in one sitting but would require blocks of time to be set aside on a regular basis. As those memoir-type stories begin to flow onto paper, there's the possibility a new realization might occur as to the purpose for their existence and the reason life is the way they find it.

I would give almost anything if my mom, my dad, grandfathers, or grandmothers had taken the time to write about their lives while they were still alive. It would be extremely interesting to now be able to read about their feelings and know what they experienced on their long journey through life. For the most part, I know nothing about any of my grandparents. The last one of the four died more than fifty-two years ago while I was still a teenager. I have strong memories of both my parents, and remember many conversations, as they taught me while growing up and through mid-life. It's now been long enough since they both died, that I'd like to have something in written form in which they could be remembered.

Maybe the books I've created in the last few years, including five separate memoirs, will be appreciated by my two children and two grandchildren, sometime in the future. Those literary works have been fun to complete, with many long hours spent at the computer. If nothing more, they've already served their purpose by satisfying me. I've learned much about myself during the process.

If you find yourself easily bored, remember what I've said about the 'joy of writing.' You can easily become an author you'll be proud of. Just sit down and start typing on your computer. Once started, stick with it. You'll surprise yourself with what can be produced, and your children and grandchildren will certainly be pleased to read about your interesting life.

Awareness

For some unknown reason, I caught myself looking around this morning at my surroundings in a completely different way than usual. I could feel myself, for just a short while, slowing down physically and mentally focusing on a few objects that are normally ignored.

While staring through a window in our kitchen, I observed a small marsh sparrow as it flittered from one branch to another in a small, red maple tree only twenty feet away. It seemed to be finding a few insects to eat, especially spiders, that were aggressively snatched from webs which were still wet from the early morning dew and reflected sunlight.

By itself, that scene didn't seem so unusual, but as I turned my head more to the right, there was something else taking place that briefly grabbed my attention. A gray squirrel on the ground, positioned just inside our brick retaining wall, had begun to chew on a pinecone that recently fell from a large tree. A second squirrel, probably its mate, rushed over and snatched the pinecone before quickly running away. Both animals were gone in an instant as they disappeared around the side of our house.

To my surprise, there was also a rabbit crouched in a stand of green grass, which was busy chewing one blade after another, as fast as he could get them in his mouth. He seemed to have no fear of the other living things moving around in the same area.

A yellow and black swallowtail butterfly, busy making its rounds on the buds of crimson-colored flowers I'd planted a month earlier, moved from plant to plant. Gathering nectar for use as energy, in preparation of laying eggs for the next generation, which had to be part of its motivation. The brilliant color contrast between that gorgeous insect and the beautiful flowers was overly impressive. It was intensified by rays of bright sunshine that flowed from a cloudless, blue sky.

I stood still and continued to stare, as questions ran through my mind. *Why don't I take the time each day to be even more aware of the simple things going on around me? Why do those creature's activities so interest me on this particular morning? Is it important that I'm here, at this very moment, observing their activities?*

It was immediately clear that those questions would require some deeper thinking for a greater understanding. I'll offer a few brief thoughts about each of them, just as they came to me.

To start with, I feel it's important to take time to 'smell the roses,' but I usually find myself not doing it often enough. For me to gain the most benefit, I must begin regarding that mental activity as essential in order to aid me in getting the most out of life. Mental focus and a keen sense of awareness are both necessary elements.

In response to the second question, it might seem I was overly interested in my surroundings on only one particular morning, but in fact, I try to regularly catch myself being an astute observer of simple things. What others seem to miss are important to me. I'm aware not everyone is that way, because we're all individuals focused on our own special interests.

To address my third question, I feel it's significant that I was present and got to see the events which were earlier described. There are some things in life that are just worth observing and being a part of. We've all heard the saying, "If a tree falls in the forest, and no one is around to hear the noise, does it actually make a sound?" In my case, I'd respond with, "Yes, and I'd rather be there to see, hear, and know what happened." It's all about individual perspective and the way we view life.

So as to have this short story include a bit more depth, I've researched the subject of 'awareness' in a few books I've read and also on the Internet. The following are quotes taken from those books, and some directly from a few individuals, with credit given to those responsible. I found them all interesting in different ways. Hopefully, you will too, as 'food for thought.'

"Look at everything, always, as though you were seeing it either for the first time or the last. This is your time on earth, and it should be filled with glory."
Betty Smith…*A Tree Grows in Brooklyn*

"It's all a matter of paying attention, being awake in the present moment, and not expecting a huge payoff. The magic in this world seems to work in whispers and small kindnesses."
Charles de Lint

"You don't need a college degree to become one of the people who knows what is really going on. If you pay attention, you can pick things up on your own."
Jennette Walls…*The Glass Castle*

"Awareness requires living in the here and now, and not in the elsewhere, the past, or the future."
Eric Berne…*Games People Play*

"If today 'is not' your day, then be happy, for this day shall never return. And, if today 'is' your day, then be happy now, for this day shall never return."
Kamand Kojouri

"If you're always racing to the next moment, what happens to the one you're in? Slow down and enjoy the moment you're in and live your life to the fullest."
Nanette Mathews

"We all have an inner voice, our personal whisper from the universe. All we have to do is listen, feel, and sense it with an open heart. Sometimes it whispers of intuition or precognition. Other times, it whispers an awareness, a remembrance from another plane. Dare to listen. Dare to hear with your heart."
C. J. Heck…*Bits and Pieces: Short Stories from a Writer's Soul*

"If you 'don't' have a high awareness, all streets are just streets; if you 'do' have a high awareness, all streets are a magic box. The world only gets bigger when your look at it deepens."
Mehmet Murat Ildan

Bloom Where You're Planted

During the year of 1999, my life took an unexpected turn in a direction I'd not previously planned. There were a host of traumatic life changes that presented themselves which included my navigating through an emotional divorce, retiring from a thirty-two-year career, changing residences, and eventually moving to another state to begin anew.

Previously, I'd always considered myself to be a stable person, able to handle adversity while working hard to provide for and raise a family. But...the sudden upheaval in my life forced me to make a host of difficult decisions and helped me realize that major roadblocks are not the end of life's journey.

While all of that turmoil was taking place, I had a meaningful conversation with my younger brother, Jim, who offered what turned out to be valuable advice. He said to me, "Ed...what you need to do is accept what has happened as an opportunity for the future and not view it as the tragedy it seems to be at this moment. Continue with your life and start doing fun and interesting things that you didn't think you had time for in the past. Heck...you're a creative person and still quite young. Get yourself a few new hobbies. Go out and meet new people. Before you know it, life will be back to normal. That will include a 'new normal,' but probably better."

Before our conversation ended, the last and best piece of advice he gave me was a statement I've never forgotten. He said, "Above all, bloom where you're planted."

Those last six words required me to think for a short time to fully absorb what was really being said. I knew I'd heard that same expression before but had never given it much serious thought. Until then, there'd really been no need for me to dwell on it or consider the logic behind its simple words.

I figured Jim knew what he was saying because he'd already been through two divorces. Each one had changed him as a person and caused major life adjustments to occur. If anyone knew what they were talking about, it had to be him.

As the following days and weeks passed, I couldn't get those words off my mind. It became a driving force in how I began to live. My daily priorities shifted and that caused me to get more involved in interesting activities within the community, develop creative interests, form new friendships, and join a few clubs and organizations. All of that newfound freedom of time led to a state of happiness beyond what I'd previously thought possible. It was very positive.

Before long, a subtle feeling of pride developed, having to do with the fact I'd been able to overcome what I'd been through. I began to regard my new experiences as a gift. If I'd not gone through all of the trauma and change, I don't believe I'd ever have had the chance to enjoy the last half of my life in the same fulfilling way.

Almost on a weekly basis now, those six words of wisdom run back through my mind. That doesn't sound very profound, but we're talking about a conversation which took place twenty-five years in the past. The impact it had on me, over the long haul, is not only a reminder of how resilient we all are as individuals, but how a simple change in attitude can affect our ultimate outcome, as we navigate through this life.

What Would You Do if You Knew Today Would be the Last Day of Your Life?

For some reason I couldn't get the above thought, the title of this story, out of my mind this morning. That unusual question seemed to linger far too long until it eventually caused me to start asking a few random people along with a couple of friends to let me know their feelings about it. I'd quickly formed a few opinions on my own but was eager to hear what others had to say.

At the beginning of my conversation when asking each of those people, I felt compelled to first give a reason for my inquiry, due to the fact my request was so unusual and a little off-the-wall. Once that was done, almost everyone hesitated for a moment before readily offering an answer that was thought-provoking for me. That's what I had expected to receive but was somewhat surprised with a few of the answers.

The first woman I asked was someone I'd known for a number of years, and I knew she possessed a strong faith and belief in God. Without hesitation, she replied, "I'd get into an intense talk with the Man, right away. I do that every day as it is in my daily prayers, but your question would call for an urgency I've never faced in the past.

I'll have to admit I'd be anxious to the point of being quite nervous. Intense prayer would be the main thing I'd suggest. To try and put myself in harmony with the spiritual power which is greater than all of us would be very important. That's the only way I can see myself ever achieving a state of peace and being able to deal with the situation you're suggesting."

I viewed her honest response as an outstanding answer to my question. Early that morning, I'd rationalized that I would also take a similar course of action, but with the clear and concise way she'd stated her personal feelings, I couldn't help but be impressed.

Some of the other individuals I approached offered a variety of both very serious and nearly-impossible-to-accomplish responses. Those that were almost impossible included things that could not be accomplished easily during their last day. I'll give you a few examples of those, so you'll understand what I'm saying.

One fellow said, "I'd go out and do something I've always wanted to do but was afraid it might kill me in the process. That would be to go skydiving. It's been my biggest fear that I've wanted to overcome for a long time. Once completed, I know I'd feel like I'd really achieved something special in my lifetime."

What I realized by his statement was that he'd certainly have to work that out very quickly in order to fit it into his schedule before his final day ended.

Another lady stated, "I'd make a point to apologize, with a few phone calls, to some of the people I know I've wronged, and I'd make a point of forgiving a few other people who I've felt wronged me."

Her answer to my question took me by complete surprise. What she'd said had a great deal of merit in accomplishing something worthy, but why in the world had she not already carried through with both of those things in the past? *Why carry the burden of those toxic feelings throughout most of your life?* I thought.

Another man told me, "I'd help out a special charity of my choice. I don't have any children and my wife died a few years ago. The money I've been saving for a rainy day should go to the benefit of a worthy cause. Yes…that's what I'd do."

One additional lady responded by saying, "I'd become an organ and tissue donor. Once I'm gone, I'll have no need for my organs anymore. I'll donate them and help someone special be able to live a long and fulfilling life."

A few of the other answers I entirely agreed with, given to me by two different people, included statements such as, "I'd try to gather my family together, those who live close by, and make sure I hugged and kissed each of them. I'd tell each one I loved them and tell them how important they'd been in my life." "I'd go directly to a local church and sit quietly in the pew to pray. I'd want to enter the last day of my life with peace and happiness in my heart. I'd want to acknowledge the beauty and perfection of this sacred moment and know that it is a true treasure."

Mahatma Gandi, a great philosopher and highly respected religious leader from India, made the statement, "Live today as if you might die tomorrow. Do this every day."

I believe he's got something there. If we live each day as if it's the last, there might be no real rush for us to take care of anything in particular during those final hours.

Time Travel

While engaged in conversation with three of my nineteen-year-old friends, one of the guys suggested we meet at a local bar to have a few beers later in the evening. That sounded good to me, so we disbursed and agreed to reassemble at John's Bar, a popular hangout located within a mile of the university at seven o'clock. By the time I got there, it was completely dark with a little snow and ice still on the ground. After exiting my car, I somehow slipped and slid my way through the paved parking lot without falling on my butt. That was quite an accomplishment for which I was thankful.

Once inside, I found the other guys who'd already claimed a wooden table near the center of the room. Our first round of beers was ordered from a good-looking waitress who moved effortlessly from one table to the next. John, the owner, stopped by and gave us a friendly 'hello' shortly afterwards. Before long, we were laughing and having a good time telling jokes and talking about some of the more interesting girls in our college classes. Everyone seemed to have a different favorite.

Just as I finished describing the gal that I found most attractive, who usually sat right behind me in biology class, into the bar she walked. With a wave of her hand and a pretty smile on her face, she marched right over and asked if she could sit with us. I was shocked by her self-confidence and willingness to introduce herself and join the gang with such little hesitation. She called me by name and pulled her chair up close.

"Aren't you gonna buy a nice girl a drink, so I can be part of the fun?" she asked me, while leaning in my direction.

"Sure. How 'bout we start with one of the same drinks I'm enjoying. Is that okay?"

"You bet. Aren't you the handsome guy who sits in the seat just in front of me in biology class?"

"Yeah. I really didn't think you'd noticed me. Thanks for the compliment. I'm thrilled you're here. What's your name?"

"I'm Wendy. Sort of like the breeze outside."

"I'm Ed. Consider me one of your admirers. Would you like to go outside and sit in my car and listen to the radio? That way we won't have to be bothered with these other guys and can talk privately."

"I'd like that very much. Let me get my beer, and we'll head in that direction."

Just as that was said, I turned over in my bed and opened my eyes. It had all been part of a strange dream going way back in time. I had to shake my head to realize that a good-looking babe would not be going to my car with me.

After coming to that realization, I calmly settled down and eventually fell back asleep.

The next thing I knew, I was playing tennis with a thirty-year-old, blonde woman who had legs that just wouldn't quit. Her tennis outfit left nothing to my imagination. She was smiling and playing like a professional, as she kept complimenting me on my elevated skill level. She was a girl after my heart, for sure. I was surprised at her interest in me, since I was about ten years older than her, at the age of roughly forty.

She asked, "Why don't we sit down for a little while and just talk? I want to get to know you better."

"Sounds good to me."

With that said, we stepped off the court and found a small table with two chairs in the shade. Before long we were deep in conversation with one personal question flowing right after the other. Within fifteen minutes, she'd told me enough about herself that I felt I'd known her for most of my life. I had also opened up to her, almost to the point of embarrassment.

We were attracted to each other, there was no question.

She asked, "Would you be interested in coming over to my

place tonight? I live alone. We could have a drink or two and then see where it takes us."

"Gosh, I don't know. Isn't that moving a little fast? How 'bout we just go to dinner and call it a night?"

"Well...I don't like to waste time, so you be the judge. Do you want to come over or not?"

"Since you put it that way, how can I resist? What time?"

"How about six o'clock? Here's my address. I'm writing it on a card, so you won't forget. See you there at six tonight."

My heart was beating double its normal speed, just as I woke up. It was the second time that night I'd had a crazy dream that had carried me back to a fictional time which had never taken place. I thought, *"Why is it that our dreams can seem so vivid and real, while our minds don't pick up on time periods that obviously don't coincide with actual reality?"*

After that second journey back into a past that never happened, but seemed to be very appealing, I again shook my head. Just before falling back to sleep for the third time, I had to remind myself that I was seventy-four years old and way too old for what I'd been dreaming about. How in the world I'd believed the two previous events had ever taken place was a mystery to me. Those were a couple of unexpected trips through time that could only happen in a dream.

I can hardly wait until tomorrow night...

Be humble and set realistic goals.
Develop a spontaneous sense of humor and use it often.
Retain a strong love of family and friends.

These are but a few important elements
which can lead to peace and contentment,
allowing you to live in a state of harmony
while surrounded by a confused and uncertain world.

Ed Hearn

A Morning Ritual

To write a short story about the following subject may seem a little boring, but stay with me, there's a purpose to my madness. Sometimes there can be a degree of depth and insight hidden in very simple things.

Over the many years of my career while working as a salesperson and part-owner in a demanding business, I felt a need each day to present myself, as far as my physical appearance, in the best light possible. Therefore, every morning, part of my routine was to take ten minutes to shave my face. It was a chore I didn't look forward to but was as necessary as brushing my teeth and other grooming activities.

My first encounter with a razor occurred around the age of twelve. Up to that time, I'd watched my dad lather up his face, first thing in the morning, and carefully shave as he stared into the mirror. It seemed to be a required ritual and part of being a grown-up man. For me, there was the feeling of urgency to get started. My problem was that both cheeks only contained a light covering of peach fuzz.

Despite that situation, I asked Dad, "When can I use your razor to shave my face?"

I'll never forget his response.

He lovingly said, "Ed, don't get started any sooner than necessary. When I was your age, I was also in a hurry to feel like a man and not a child. I'd watched your granddad shave each morning and longed for the opportunity to do the same. I was sure once that began, I'd no longer be considered a kid."

Dad followed up that statement with some well-intentioned advice, by saying, "Don't be in a rush to get started. Once those fine hairs are trimmed, coarser hairs will start growing in their place. That will continue for the rest of your life. You'll have plenty of opportunities to shave your face. Just don't begin before it's entirely necessary."

I thought about what Dad had said for the rest of that day. It all made good sense, but while staring into the mirror the next morning, I could wait no longer. Soon after Dad left for work, I used his can of white foam and spread the stuff all over my face. I figured using his razor and lightly trimming the fuzz wouldn't hurt anything. Boy, was I wrong. That was the beginning of a lifetime of shaving because the course hair that followed just wouldn't quit growing.

Many years later and shortly following retirement, a shift was made in my personal hygiene schedule where I felt the routine of shaving was only necessary every other day. I discovered after the first day that the short stubble which had grown overnight could be tolerated a bit longer, because my main goal was just to be comfortable. No longer did I have to meet and talk with customers, which required looking my best. However, once two days had passed without shaving, I couldn't stand the whiskers and had to get rid of them.

All of what I've mentioned so far, including the early interaction with my dad, has been told to carry me into the rest of my story.

By the age of seventy-four, my dad was suffering from congestive heart failure. He'd already experienced two separate, nearly fatal episodes where excess fluid accumulation around his heart and in his lungs had cut off the flow of oxygen. After collapsing and becoming unconscious, followed by turning blue, he was only saved each time by a quick response from paramedics. They administered a strong diuretic drug which quickly removed some of the liquid in his chest, allowing him to breathe again. Both were close calls.

When I went to the hospital to visit him the evening after his second near-death experience, he looked up at me from his bed and said, "Ed, you almost lost me this time. After I regained consciousness, the doctor told me that if I'd not been given that special diuretic drug, within a couple of minutes I would have been dead. The paramedics arrived just in time."

"Dad, I'm so glad you're alive. I love you and don't want to lose you. Why don't you get some rest, and I'll see you in the morning."

Instead of being sent home after that second occurrence, Dad was transferred to a private room in the hospital. He stayed there for two weeks and was then moved to a separate nursing facility so technicians could continue monitoring him with around-the-clock care.

My younger brother, sister, and I each stayed with him for eight-hour shifts in rotation. We didn't want him to be alone. That schedule was tough on everyone. Dad grew increasingly tired and tended to sleep most of the time due to the heavy doses of drugs he was being given.

After two weeks of him remaining in the nursing facility, and during my time to be there, I asked one evening, "Dad, you've got a light growth of beard on your face. Would you like me to shave it off? I'm sure you'll feel much better without all that bristly, coarse hair on your face."

"Yes…I'd like that very much," he said.

Very carefully I applied his favorite shaving cream to his face and used a razor that were both stored in his small bathroom. While working, I stared into his eyes as he faced me while sitting in his chair near the edge of the bed. As I cautiously moved that razor up and down his cheeks and neck, I couldn't help but think back to many years earlier when we had that first conversation about shaving. He was right back then. Once the shaving chore begins, it goes on for the rest of your life.

I finished, cleaned up his face with a warm towel, and asked, "How do you feel now, Dad?"

He replied, "That feels so much better. Thank you, son."

My eight-hour shift ended a few hours later, and I left to get back to work after giving him a light kiss on the cheek. My sister relieved me and took over the job. A long hard day at the office followed.

It was the last time I saw my dad alive. He died suddenly the next day.

I've often thought about that final shave I gave him. I didn't focus on it at the time, but when I looked into his eyes while shaving his face, I knew he loved me. That thought has stayed with me now for almost twenty-eight years. He was a good man and a good father.

Honoring My Older Brother

While growing up during the 1950s, my four-year older brother Travis forged the way for many of my personal discoveries, adventures, and later successes. I regularly looked up to him and relied on his judgment and direction. Because of his desire to pursue a variety of different interests, I was included and exposed to much more than if I'd been an only child.

Together, we attended Cub Scout meetings in the neighborhood that our mom conducted as the den mother, in spite of the fact I was actually too young to be included at the time. Usually there'd be around fifteen of us present and each week a new and different project would be worked through. Sometimes it was as simple and making octagonal bowls out of a bunch of popsicle sticks, carving something interesting using bars of soap and a small knife, building a crude battery-driven Morris-code device, making decorative lanyards to wear around our necks out of colored gimp, stitching leather wallets together made from tanned animal hides, forming cloth booties from old cotton wash cloths, plus a large number of other intriguing activities. I was always thrilled to be involved with the older guys and looked up to my brother because he'd help me complete whatever I was attempting to achieve. Mixed in with all of those varied crafts, we somehow found time to study a furnished workbook and move from one level to the other to finally graduate as full-fledged Boy Scouts.

Outside of those organized weekly gatherings, the two of us started our own stamp collections, with him ordering sample packs of foreign stamps for no more than fifty cents per shipment, from The Littleton Stamp Company that advertised nationwide.

As a result of my accumulating an extensive collection, I learned important details about the existence of other countries throughout the world. Somewhere along the line, he shifted to collecting mainly United States stamps going back to the early 1800s, and I'm sure that collection, which his older son now owns almost seventy years later, is quite valuable.

Later, we both started collecting coins. At first it was just copper pennies, then nickels and silver dimes. During our earlier search for old pennies, we'd get our dad to stop by the bank on a Saturday morning where we'd exchange our individual weekly allowance of only a dollar into rolls of pennies. Those would be looked through carefully for the dates and marked mint locations we didn't already have in our collections, followed by us proudly placing them in individual folders. There's no telling how many coins of various denominations the two of us went through together before I turned ten years old, as we added to those collections. At this time, my younger son owns all of those coins I amassed long ago.

After I reached the age of eight, Travis and I built so many plastic model airplanes and one-twenty-fifth-scale cars that at one point those highly detailcd and colorful completed items were scattered all over our house. Every end table, coffee table, dresser-top, and available space held one or more of our creations. Usually, there were two or three in each of those locations.

On the weekends, he'd take me along with a couple of his other buddies, as we walked almost a mile down a side road to see the Saturday evening matinee movie at the local cinema. Along the way, I usually talked too much and was told to keep my mouth shut if I wanted to be invited for the next outing. I did as he asked.

When it came time to learn how to play with either a butterfly yoyo or circular hula hoop during 1957, he was my teacher. We had competitions in the neighborhood to see who could accomplish the most innovative tricks using a yoyo or who could last the longest in keeping the hula hoop rotating around our waists. Between the two of us, he won most of the time, but I always gave it my best effort.

Whenever the neighborhood gang would gather in our side lot to play baseball, Travis made sure I was included. I'd be put in the outfield because he knew I couldn't catch a ball that had been hit hard, but I could run and fetch it before it went across the narrow road which ran in front of our small house.

During 1961, Travis decided to supplement his regular high school education by taking a vocational subject offered to anyone interested at our school. By doing so, he entered the world of printing and publishing. That one decision by him ended up changing the course of our entire family. The school had a very large manufacturing facility on campus with a full staff of instructors who taught around one hundred interested students how to run presses and produce a usable printed product. Each involved student took normal book classes for one half of each school day and would then enter the world of printing for the other half. Because the school we attended was supported by the State of Tennessee, its printing plant produced the materials used by government offices throughout the state. That included all of its counties, and the State Capitol located in downtown Nashville.

I followed Travis with that decision by taking printing classes starting at the beginning of my ninth-grade year, and our younger brother Jim later did the same. Once we finished college, each of us used that profession to form our individual careers. Those jobs eventually expanded to involve our wives, children, and some of the grandchildren in the same profession.

Much earlier and while still in high school, Travis ventured out and became a member of the high school basketball team during his ninth-grade year. Once he realized that each day's practice involved constantly running up and down the court, he stopped that activity after only a few weeks. As I look back on it now, by him having broken the barrier of stepping out into a brand-new area, that of high school sports, it led me to later join the basketball team while I was in junior high, where I played consistently on all the teams throughout every year from the seventh to twelfth grade. I was forever grateful to him for doing that, even though he never really knew it. I actually played for a while with my college basketball team during my freshman year as a result of my earlier successes with our high school team.

Another of Travis' life-changing decisions, which indirectly resulted in affecting me, came when he joined our high school track and field team. As he matured into a very strong physical person, during the years from early 1961 through the spring of 1963, he ended up setting records with the shot-put event that no one at the school broke until our youngest brother Jim finally achieved that goal during his senior year in 1969. For me, I was part of the track team for four years but finished just shy of the other two brothers' achievements with that particular event during high school.

Where Travis truly excelled during his high school years was in him being a major part of our football team. He became a dominant right tackle, playing both offensive and defensive positions, and was feared by all opponents. By leading our winning team to an end-of-the-season Bowl game during November of 1962, he was given an athletic scholarship to later play football in college.

All of his successful sports involvement opened the door, leading me to a world that would change my life forever. Throughout all four years of high school, I played basketball, was part of the track and field team, and successfully played football, all with many personal achievements. At the end of my high school senior year, I was awarded the honor of 'All-City Player of the Year' for my accomplishments as a right tackle on our team. During college, I was awarded a full-grant athletic scholarship for four years to be part of the track and field team, which ultimately resulted in many nationwide successes. On into my sixties, I continued my quest for achievement in that sport while gaining multiple honors that were never expected. I owe all of those achievements to my older brother.

Travis started his working career during 1966 by becoming a manager of a large department store in Cookeville, Tennessee, the same town in which the college was located. At that time, he was married, had a young son, and was still a full-time student. He no longer played football on scholarship. He continued working for that same business, after being transferred multiple times to different cities in Kentucky, Tennessee and Alabama to help open new stores in its expanding chain throughout the southeast, until it finally went bankrupt in 1979. That was a complete shock for him and his family. He'd given that business all his time and energy for almost thirteen years, usually working seven days a week, always being told the best was yet to come.

Out of complete bewilderment, he moved back to Nashville and took a job with our younger brother's printing company selling printing products. Being an outdoor salesman, with its inherent stresses, never seemed to fit Travis' personality. He struggled with it for around five years until finally leaving and searching for another way to make a living.

Early on, while he was working for our younger brother, his wife of seventeen years decided to leave him for another man. She left him with two children, ages twelve and fourteen, which he had to take care of by himself. After working just a few months each for three different companies, all in outdoor sales, Travis ended up accepting a job with the same business I'd worked with for the past eighteen years.

On July 5th of 1988, Travis became an inside employee working with me, where he oversaw a section of our printing production. I was glad to again be able to see and talk with him on a daily basis. That hadn't been possible in many years.

To give a little more background information, Travis had suffered with panic attacks and anxiety starting in 1984 due to the high level of stress he personally experienced being an outdoor salesman, plus his added family problems. His health concerns became so bad that a few times he thought he was having a heart attack. That resulted in him being taken to the emergency room by ambulance to be evaluated on more than one occasion.

Those crisis events took a toll on him, with the doctors doing expensive tests and ultimately telling him he was okay. Because of embarrassment and money he owed, that he didn't have, he vowed to never again go to either a doctor or hospital.

One Monday morning around the summer of 1998, Travis approached me with an unusual situation. He showed me his forearm, revealing an intensely red circle of about four inches in diameter, that had become visible a day earlier. At the same time, he told me he'd been cutting bamboo poles to use for fishing the previous Friday. When he left the wooded area, he explained that a small tick was attached to his forearm in the exact center of the place that was now very inflamed. He'd simply pulled the tick loose and tossed it on the ground.

Immediately I recognized it as the sign of a serious virus transferred by ticks called Lyme's Disease. I said to him, "Travis, you've got Lyme's Disease. There's no question in my mind about it. You're showing the exact symptoms of having been bitten by an infected tick. It's Monday, you need to take off work, go to your doctor, and start taking shots of antibiotics to get it out of your system. It's very serious and nothing to take lightly. With about a month's worth of treatments, you'll be fine."

His response was shocking, "Ed, I'm okay. I just wanted to show you the red circle on my arm because it was unusual. I'll be fine. I'm not going to the doctor for any treatments."

As he walked away, I could hardly believe it. He had always been stubborn as a mule, but this was insane on his part. For the next few days, I didn't say anything to him about the issue, expecting him to eventually come to his senses and go to the doctor. That never happened.

After eight days, the red circle completely disappeared. He

approached me with the news and said, "Quit worrying about me. The red circle has gone away. Everything is fine."

All I could think to say was, "You're not fine. That harmful virus is now in your system. You must get treatment to get rid of it. That won't happen naturally. Take off work and go to the doctor."

He again just walked away with the comment, "I'm not going to the doctor."

The weeks and months went by and every day, Monday through Friday, I begged him to go get treatment for the Lyme's Disease I knew was working havoc inside his body. Every time I said something about it, he declined, and said, "I'm fine. Leave me alone and quit bringing it up."

For the next eight months, I continued to bring it up on a regular basis, only to get the same feedback.

Finally, he said out of disgust, "Don't ever talk about the Lyme's Disease issue again. I'm tired of your bugging me about it."

When he said that, I let it go for a year or so. Afterwards, he always looked tired to me, but I thought he was dealing with so many different pressures in his life that the reason for it was something else. One day I walked up to him and asked, "How are you feeling? You look tired."

His response was, "Yes…I'm tired. I've not been able to sleep well at night. For the last three months I've had a constant headache that won't go away. Day and night my head throbs, and it keeps me from being able to get a good night's rest. I wake up tired every morning after just a short nap."

All I could say in return was the truth. "Travis, you've got Lyme's Disease. It's a very serious condition. You must go to the doctor for treatment to ever get rid of it. According to what I've read, that virus gets into your organs and causes major problems."

"You've told me that same thing over and over. The red circle went away a long time ago, and I'm fine. Leave me alone."

I did as he asked for another few months, until one day I asked him again how he was feeling. He said, "My joints have begun to ache...and my back hurts constantly. The headache still hasn't gone away. It's driving me crazy. I'm tired all the time."

"You know what I'm going to say, don't you?"

"Yes...you're going to tell me to go to the doctor, which I'm not going to do."

That went on for another long period of time, until the virus had worked its way into his brain. He began having serious issues with his balance. He'd be talking and start falling sideways, hitting the floor on his side, never knowing he was off balance.

By that time, he knew he was in trouble. Finally a doctor's appointment was made. When he sat down and explained some of the symptoms he was experiencing, his doctor asked, "Do you have any idea what's the problem?"

"My brother has been telling me for years that I have Lyme's Disease. Do you think that would cause these kind of health issues for me?"

"Certainly. That's a very serious disease. Let me run some tests, and I'll let you know the results. We can do a few of the more important ones today while you wait."

"Sure. Let's do that. I'll give you blood and wait for the results. I've got to get rid of whatever is happening to me."

About an hour later, the doctor had Travis come back into one of the rooms and take a seat. He sat down beside him and said, "Yes...your brother was right. You have Lyme's Disease, and you've had it for a long time. So long that it's now spread throughout your entire body involving all your major organs. It's also in your brain. That's why you're having balance problems and falling. I'm sorry to say that you don't have long to live. I'd advise you to go home and get your things in order, because I don't give you longer than about three months before you'll be dead."

That took Travis by complete surprise. He thought with

modern medicine, the doctor would be able to correct the problem, even though he'd waited way too long.

By that time, Travis was no longer able to work. He spent each day at home, never able to get a full night's sleep. I went to visit him at his home just a few weeks before his death on July 1st, 2006. We sat in lawn chairs on a concrete porch outside his house to get out of the sun. During our conversation, he was only able to talk and concentrate for a few minutes at a time. In the very middle of a sentence, he'd fall asleep, only to wake after a brief moment of silence. That went on the entire time we were together.

After about an hour, I knew he was exhausted. I decided to leave so he could get some rest. When I walked to my car, he followed. He stopped me, looked into my eyes, and said, "Ed, I love you."

What he said took me by surprise. All I could think was to return the statement. "Travis, you know I love you also. I hope you get to feeling better."

It was the last time I saw him alive. He died a little more than three months after finally visiting the doctor.

Shelby Park

On the east side of the city of Nashville, Tennessee, there's a charming little area known as Shelby Park. That land of approximately one thousand and two hundred acres borders the winding Cumberland River, which runs past the north edge of downtown Nashville. The river comes very close to the end of Broadway Street and ultimately flows all the way to the Mississippi River near Memphis, approximately two hundred miles in the distance. An older neighborhood of mostly siding-covered homes was built on small lots surrounding the park during the 20s and 30s. Many of them are still standing and in reasonably good shape after nearly one hundred years.

Shelby Park consists of a large number of well-maintained baseball and softball diamonds with numerous lights mounted on tall poles for late evening play. Under a long line of nearby trees, there's a series of covered stone and concrete shelters located to the side with picnic tables and permanent charcoal grills for use by Nashville's citizens and visitors. On a Saturday evening, it's not unusual to see as many as twenty grills putting out a constant stream of white smoke while steaks, hamburgers, and hot dogs are being cooked. The inviting smell will always make your mouth water.

Years ago, because our family didn't have much money to spend on those type of meats, Mom and Dad would usually take a picnic basket full of inexpensive items, such as sliced baloney or canned spam, complimented with fresh lettuce and tomatoes that had been grown in our garden, a jar of mayonnaise, and always a loaf of white bread made by the Colonial Baking Company in Nashville in order to make sandwiches. Coca Cola in small, dark glass bottles was always the drink of choice, along with a big bag of potato chips to round out the meal. We generally used one of the picnic tables to enjoy our feast, and seldom used the accompanying grill.

A manicured golf course has always been part of that setting, which is surrounded by huge, old-growth hardwood trees. Looking around, all that's seen are undulating, rolling hills and green vegetation everywhere. Its nature on display at its finest. Off to one side, and spanning the Cumberland River, stands an old railroad bridge that has stood for more than a century. That black metal structure is iconic from a time in the past when steam engine locomotives carried freight through the area and delivered it to many places around the South.

One of the other interesting parts of the park is a large body of water known as Shelby Park Lake. It has consistently had its share of pet mallard ducks and white hybrid geese that always seem to be cruising around looking for food. Many of the families who visit that lake with their children will bring scraps of bread and crackers to feed those birds. During the 50s and 60s, there were paddle boats for rent near an old wooden dock with a kind gentleman in charge. I don't know if the dock is still there today. He made sure a life jacket was worn by everyone who boarded one of his boats and gave the same safety instructions over and over to each person.

As a kid, I can remember my parents taking our family to that lake on a few Saturday mornings to fish off its mud and stone-lined shore. All we needed was a box of worms for bait, our rods, a collection of white and red floats, and our tackle boxes that contained extra hooks with split-shot weights.

About once a year, there would be a competitive fishing tournament sponsored by the local newspaper and the city. It brought out hundreds of younger fishing enthusiasts who were all interested in enjoying a few hours of leisure time with their parents on a warm summer day. Awards were given for the biggest fish of a specified species and to the kid who caught the largest number of fish overall. Usually, the winners were photographed, and their smiling faces were shown in the next day's newspaper in black and white with a short story. One year, when I was only seven and my younger brother Jim was five, our photo was taken together and appeared in the paper as we each held up two small fish that were still connected to our individual lines. We'd been credited as catching the most fish, with the help of our dad, on that day.

About that same time, during the mid-1950s, there was a long, paved ramp that ran at a steep slant down a hillside of the Cumberland River at the edge of Shelby Park, which led to an old wooden, flatbottomed ferryboat that carried cars and people from one side to the other. To take the ferry was considered a short cut which got you to the other side of the river much faster than driving to a whole different place that was many miles away.

When I think about crossing that river on the ferry, what sticks out most in my mind was the long line of cars that seemed to always be waiting patiently to be loaded for the next trip across. Once the ferry arrived on the other side, maybe a distance of around four hundred yards, there was a delay of approximately twenty-five minutes or more as the cars and people slowly unloaded before the men in charge allowed the next waiting group who were going in the opposite direction to be loaded. It was not uncommon for us to wait up to an hour to complete the entire journey across, but we did it mostly for enjoyment and the uniqueness of traveling that way, not as a necessity.

My place of business, where I worked for over thirty years in the East Nashville area, was no more than three miles from Shelby Park. During the very early 1970s, shortly after graduating from college, I made it a regular outing during the summer months to bring my lunch to work in a brown paper bag and drive to the park around noon to sit on the edge of a picnic table while enjoying the surroundings in peace and quiet. There were squirrels everywhere and usually a few bike riders. Lots of birdlife filled the trees. It was a restful experience that took me away from the stress of the job for about forty-five minutes, which I looked forward to on a regular basis.

Early fall was especially nice in the park. Once the trees started to turn colors, with their oranges, yellows, and reds, combined with the coolness in the air and lack of excess humidity, it was the place to be.

As I look back on those times now, having lived on the east coast of the United States for the past twenty-four years, I miss those moments of reflection and quiet solitude that were spent in Shelby Park so long ago. I believe the next time I'm in Nashville, I'll make a point to stop by and see how much the place has changed. I'm sure many parts of it will be different. What I've found is that no matter where you are very little seems to remain the same after a few years have passed.

Old Photos

There's nothing much better than taking a few hours of idle time to flip through a stack of old family photos that had originally been created on photographic print paper. With most everyone these days storing their photographic images on a digital computer's hard drive or on a separate computer disc to be later viewed on a screen, I don't think that more modern experience is nearly the same. For me, it's just like being able to sit down and read a heartwarming novel from a hardback book. I love to hold the glossy, black and white or color photos in my hand and view them carefully, as past memories flood through my mind. I can linger on each one as long as necessary and give it the time it deserves.

With each image viewed, there's usually a memory or two that easily transports me to an earlier time in my life. Most of those bring back positive thoughts, but some can carry along negative remembrances based on what eventually happened to certain people that are pictured. Some of them became sick and died in the following years, one or two were involved in bad accidents, a few went through emotional divorces that destroyed their family life, while others seem to have just disappeared the way our friends sometimes do, as everyone drifts in different directions with the normal passage of time.

I had a chance not too long ago to sit down and slowly go through a mass of old images, as I lifted them one at a time, from a variety of cardboard boxes where they'd been stored. That was done while unpacking those boxes after having moved into a new home which was recently finished. While all the construction was taking place, we'd busied ourselves with packing our valuables and discarding many of the unusable items which had accumulated over the past twenty-four years. Saving old photographs had been high on my priority list. Therefore, a large quantity of the old photos had been quickly placed in boxes to be sorted through at a future date.

In the process of unpacking, I ran across a number of them that I valued greatly and hadn't seen in what seemed to be forever, sometimes as much as fifty or sixty years. Some of those were either already framed and ready to hang, or loosely stacked without frames, in a bunch of folders. A large selection had been mounted in various albums sometime in the distant past, but usually those were in the process of releasing from their mountings and desperately needed to be replaced in new albums.

This all brought to mind the fact that I'd seen some very old albums which had been assembled over one hundred years ago for a relative in the family. Inside, there were numerous photos, newspaper clippings and various important documents that had been preserved through the years. Much of that information was yellowed with age and somewhat brittle, but it was still readable.

I thought to myself, *If I could ever find a way to get the majority of my stuff put into nice albums, that would be a great way for it to last for many decades and long after I'm gone. I would even be willing to mount my loose photos as a way to preserve them.*

That's where my younger sister, Gail, was able to offer her valuable assistance. I knew that in total I had a couple of large boxes full of old memorabilia, including newspaper clippings and photographs going back to when I was a kid. In a discussion, she offered to organize and assemble much of that into a group of new, display albums. I was thrilled with her willingness to help in such a special way.

After weeks and weeks of hard work, she finally called and told me that a miracle had been achieved. She had completed the meticulous mounting of everything into nine different albums. Each one contained one hundred pages with a beautiful leather cover. She let me know those binders were manufactured in such a way that they'd last for many decades to come.

In response, I didn't know what to say. My appreciation for her doing all of that tedious work was overwhelming. It was something that really needed to be done for the long-term preservation of our family history, but I knew I'd never find the time to do it myself. She had made it happen for her older brother.

How much better can it get...than to have a caring sister willing to help a brother with a valuable family project. I'm proud of her.

Why Am I Feeling so Bad?

How many times have you opened your eyes in the morning and sensed that things just weren't right? Maybe you had been up late the night before and didn't get a good night's sleep. Or maybe you had eaten something unusual for supper that just didn't agree with your digestive system.

On those mornings, it would be normal to linger in bed for a while and ask yourself the question, "Why am I feeling so bad?"

That happened to me recently. When I finally decided to get up and eat breakfast, an overwhelming sensation was, "I just plain feel lousy. Now that I'm up, I don't even feel well enough to eat a morning meal. What's wrong with me?"

To get a body temperature reading was my first choice in determining the problem. Within minutes, I was looking at the numbers, and they showed my temperature was one-hundred and one degrees. I knew that was on the high side and should receive immediate attention.

My next reaction was to determine if, by chance, I had contracted Covid. It had been on the news just a few days earlier that the virus was again spreading throughout our population. One of the news programs on television had recently broadcast that a new variant was going around and spreading rapidly through the population.

I knew we had two different manufacturers' test kits in the house for Covid, so both of them were used. After following all the instructions, I was showing two solid lines on both test kits. The outcome…I definitely was positive and had the Covid virus in my body. That was a sure sign of the reason I was feeling so lousy.

Number one on the list, I knew my temperature was elevated.

That in itself will usually cause a person to not feel good. In addition, I had a slight headache. I also felt a little weakness in my shoulders, had some body chills, a few body aches, and to top it all off, a slight cough.

All I wanted to do was lay down on the couch and not be bothered by anyone. Once there, I didn't want to get up. The whole thing had hit me so quickly I could hardly believe it.

I began to run the situation through my mind and ask the question, "Where in the world did I pick up this nasty virus? I haven't been around many different people in the last few days, mostly working at home by myself. Occasionally I've gone to eat lunch at a local restaurant but have always eaten by myself and then came directly back home."

It was all so strange, I thought.

As I lay on the couch, I remembered hearing about a special drug that had just been developed by Pfizer named Paxlovid. The report I'd heard indicated that drug, in the form of pills, had been developed for the new variant of Covid and should be taken within the first few days after exhibiting outward symptoms. If taken in time, it could decrease the severity and length of time necessary for recovery.

A phone call was made to my personal doctor, where I described my symptoms in detail, along with giving her the positive results from the two different Covid tests. The next thing I knew, I had a prescription for the new drug and needed someone to go to the pharmacy for me. I was in no shape to do it myself. That pick up was arranged, and I soon had the prescription in my hands. I was told that only a five-day regiment would be issued, in that it was so strong and effective no more would be needed.

Within two days, taking three of those special pills at a time, twice a day, I began to feel better. It was an amazing turnaround. The only negative thing I can mention is that the pills leave a lingering, metallic taste in the mouth. I was told that goes away shortly after the five-day session is completed.

The really good part about this newest variant of Covid is that it's not affecting the respiratory system. Back in early 2020 and up to a year or more later, many thousands of individuals died due to breathing and respiratory problems. I experienced none of that. The concern now seems to be mainly for older people who have weak immunity systems. If the body's not capable of fighting off the virus, then this new variant is much more dangerous.

Prior to having this current problem, I'd taken all five of the previous shots, starting in late February of 2020. Apparently, the protection I gained from those shots over the last two and a half years has ended.

I'm now considered an older guy in my mid-seventies, but I still feel I'm quite healthy. What it shows is that almost anyone is susceptible. You can't be too careful. If you start showing the same symptoms that hit me, immediately call your doctor and request this new drug named Paxlovid. In my opinion, it's a miracle worker, which will allow you to feel much better in a short period of time.

Smile and try to include
a bit of humor into
each day.

It's the best way
to ease tension
and lower the
stress levels of daily life.

Ed Hearn

Viewing Ourselves and Our Physical Age

My sister, Gail, recently read a thought-provoking question in a magazine that caught her attention. It caused her to start thinking on a deeper plane, and it did the same for me. The question asked, "How old would you be if you didn't know how old you are?"

On the surface, I accepted what was asked as trivial and didn't dig too far down to get an answer. I figured the best and quickest answer would be a time during my youth. Maybe ten, fifteen, or twenty years old would be nice. A lot of what is being asked has to do with a person's view of themselves, which would include their physical health, mental state of mind, and possible aspirations of still achieving things on a potential 'bucket list" within their lifetime.

If a person's health was good, and they regularly interacted with others without any physical problems, even a ninety-year-old might view himself as very young. That perception would be optimal, and a response that would certainly be envied by most everyone else. If the person's health was bad, and they were physically limited, maybe they would view themselves as much older.

The same would be true of someone who possessed sharp mental capabilities and operated with a clear, active mind. They might see themselves on a whole different level than someone who was in obvious mental decline. To still be inquisitive, alert, and able to solve problems without hesitation would surely make that individual feel much younger than their actual physical state. At any age, to have a constantly curious and productive mind is to be admired.

To be a person always looking forward to the future, exploring options for new adventures, would certainly be someone with a youthful attitude. I know that if I were an old man of eighty-five or ninety and still interested in accomplishing a list of activities, many of them involving a physical lifestyle, I would have to view myself much younger than my actual age. In answering the question asked above, I might respond with an answer of thirty or even forty years old.

Gail responded to that same question by saying, "If I knew what I know now…I'd give an answer of eighteen. Otherwise, I'd answer the question by saying, twenty-one years old." That was an interesting answer, because to be able to take back in time what you've gained in knowledge throughout life would work to your advantage. You could use those younger years in a more advantageous way with all that you've learned and experienced up to this point.

I believe everyone would have a different answer, with most gauging it on the three personal conditions discussed above. The age you give yourself, if you didn't know how old you were, would have to be in line with your current physical condition, state of mind, and daily energy level available. All of those together allow you to be able to enjoy what the world has to offer.

Any way you look at it, the question presented is definitely worth a bit of time to process and think through carefully. It seems that each time I tell someone who asks my current age, I find myself letting that number affect how I feel about myself. Outwardly, I feel I'm much younger than my actual years indicate. That's good, for sure. If I can just continue along that same course and state of mind, I know it will benefit me greatly as additional years go by.

Keep all of this in mind the next time someone asks in casual conversation, "How old are you?" Maybe the best answer would be to give a smaller number than the truth, with a slight smile. At least you might feel better about yourself, unless your actual age doesn't bother you. That in itself could be a blessing in disguise.

Religion

Not too long ago, my younger son asked me a point-blank question. Out of nowhere, he asked, "Do you believe in God?" At first, that caught me a bit off-guard. He then went on to say, "I'm curious about your views in general. In my case, I'm unsure at this moment exactly how I feel. I believe I've been an atheist/agnostic since about the age of twelve. After having known a few individuals who recently died at or near my age, it has brought home to me how short the experience of life can really be. That and other things have made me begin to question the whole concept more seriously."

I responded by saying, "It's interesting that you ask me so bluntly, but I appreciate the question. I didn't realize you were so uncertain about the subject. First, let me say that religion, in my opinion, is a very personal thing. It means something a little different for each person. What we believe or what particular religion we may or may not follow depends a great deal on our experiences in life so far and where we were born.

For instance, if I'd been born in India, I might be a Hindu or Muslim. On the other hand, if born into a family already devoted to the Catholic religion, I may have become a Catholic. There's a lot of ceremony connected with that particular religion and a more outward 'show' than I feel comfortable with, so that one somewhat turns me off.

I believe most religions are about the same basic thing, which is that there's something bigger and more powerful than ourselves. Many people seem to turn to some form of religion in an effort to understand the ultimate questions about life for themselves. A few examples would be questions such as, "Why am I here?" and "What is my purpose?"

During most lifetimes, something powerful usually happens which brings a person around to searching for deeper help and greater understanding. Ultimately, there is a level of what is referred to as 'faith' which can develop from that effort. That's basically what religion is about...faith. You have to trust in something which is not visible or provable. Some individuals go through their entire lives without having a need for religion. Others can never get away from it and refuse to live without it.

My answer to your question is, "yes." I believe there's a God, but maybe not in the same sense most people think about it. For me, God is a very personal thing and bigger than life. God, to me, is not a person but a way of being. I have a personal need for there to be a God, or a special way of being, so my mindset accepts it. I don't currently attend church regularly, pray frequently, or beg God to do things for me. That doesn't mean I won't ever let that be a part of my life again. Throughout my life, I've had periods of time where I needed God and did those things. In those moments I was helped. Sometimes I didn't realize immediately I was being helped and didn't find out until later a course of events, good or bad, had taken place to lead to my ultimate betterment. Whether I actually helped myself by a particular change of mental attitude or if something else outside of me occurred, I'm not really sure. Those are some of the signs of the 'Y's' in the road I've talked about before. There are moments when life-changing decisions are made, which affect the future and can seldomly be reversed.

One of the big reasons I follow astronomy, paleontology, and the natural sciences is that I see how diverse this planet and the solar system truly are. Believing in evolution is one thing, but believing in God is a whole different element, with both being infinitely tied together.

First, I have to develop an appreciation for all there is which is visible, but second, I have to develop an appreciation for what I can't see. To be able to approach both of those at the same time, and view both as viable options, is the maximum course of action. Those who are completely turned off to considering the unseeable can easily miss a lot of what life has to offer. No one's arm can be twisted, forcing them into believing something that seems unreal. They have to come to that personal realization on their own. Many times, a person who spends most of his lifetime feeling he's an atheist, can flip completely and start considering himself a believer. It happens all the time. Some never make the change. It's all a very personal decision.

I don't push religion or my beliefs on anyone because I understand it's a big turnoff to many people for someone to be outwardly vocal, unless asked directly. As long as I'm content and at peace within my own self, that's what really matters. We're all part of a big journey, and we're all on a different path. Where we arrive or when we arrive is just part of that journey.

One of these days, you will feel the need to read some or all of the books I've personally written, because you're my son. They were all written mostly for you and your older brother, so you'd know more about your dad. I'm currently working on publishing book number fifteen. I've found, completely by accident, that hundreds and hundreds of other people have enjoyed those earlier books. That knowledge has really surprised me. There's not a day that passes when I don't have at least one person who asks me about one of my stories within those books, either by email or in person. Some of those stories are about simple foolish things, some are about humorous things, some are about facts, and some are deep inner reflections about life in general.

I just wish my parents or grandparents had taken the time to write about their lives, as I've tried to do. I would now love to sit and read about their experiences in order to know their innermost thoughts and feelings. All I have are memories of them, and many of those are somewhat distorted without knowing their true feelings about the world in which they lived. That's too bad, in my opinion. We all have a story to tell.

I believe there's a God, and I believe I'm a spiritual person.

The good thing is I know I don't have to prove it to anyone. All that really matters is what's inside me.

I hope I've given you the answer to the question you asked. It may or may not be what you wanted to hear. It's not something to argue about. You are one of God's creations, and I'm proud of you, no matter what you personally feel about God and religion at this moment. Just know that I love you.

Early Morning Mind Games

Have you ever opened your eyes in the morning, while still lying in bed, and quietly stared at the ceiling as memories from your life begin to flood through your mind? That's almost a daily occurrence for me. I find it's a prime time for inner reflection where past events get replayed so they can be more fully evaluated, many of which haven't been thought about for many years. As those images appear and briefly linger, I frequently question if I'm still dreaming or if I've already returned to reality.

One of the first things which usually comes to mind is how old I am...my current age. That topic may seem to be a little strange to deal with each morning, but for me, it's what happens. The number of years which have passed and how many I may have left are of great importance. It's almost as if I'm required to seriously consider where I am in time in order to gain some degree of orientation. What day of the week is it? What's the current date? That I'm now in my mid-seventies seems to be a regular surprise. How in the world did I get so old, so fast?

Following that short analysis of my current age and its relationship to the whole spectrum of a normal lifespan, my thoughts usually switch to other items of interest. A few random memories from the distant past might start to run like an old movie where I recall being young or middle-aged while interacting with old friends and family. At first, I question if those visions are real or if they're actually only remnants from the dreamworld I've just left behind in my sleep.

For only a few waking moments, it's not uncommon to have the feeling I've just spent time with a friend or family member who I later realize no longer exists. Those people may be long gone, but within my mind, it's as if they were still alive. At other times, I begin to think about the actual dates that particular events took place with one of those individuals, and then I calculate the total number of years which have passed until the present. It always seems to amaze me when I accept the fact a few of those happenings occurred fifty or even sixty years in the past...possibly more. Time does move on, and people come and go...whether I like it or not.

After having spent valuable moments thinking about people and events from my past, I sometimes find myself mentally shifting forward in time only to wonder about what might still be left to experience in life. It causes me to ask, 'What does the future really hold?' I've never received a complete answer to that question, but that doesn't keep my mind from continuing to explore the question on a regular basis.

One more interesting thought which seems to regularly run through my head in the morning has to do with the question of what effect my existence may have had on others and possibly the world in general. Like me, I'm sure you've considered what I'm about to ask...If I'd never been born or had died at an early age, how different would the world be today? Has my presence altered the course of what would have been, thereby changing everything? I think it has.

On the surface those questions sound somewhat egotistical, but in reality, they're worth serious consideration. I've thought about them a lot over my lifetime. I can't seem to get away from the fact that every decision and action I've taken, usually with only myself in mind, has actually affected everyone else around me in some small way. The phrase, 'No man is an island,' is one I learned a long time ago. Another popular truism is, 'For every action, there is a reaction.' Those are both cliches but hit the nail right on its head with their full depth of meaning.

Almost twenty-four years ago, I moved to Wilmington, North Carolina after having called Nashville, Tennessee home for fifty years. That move followed retirement and the sale of my interest in a business where I'd been part-owner and worked for more than thirty years.

Had I not moved to North Carolina, none of the hundreds and hundreds of people I've interacted with in that new location would have known anything about me or my life. My potential influence on them, good or bad, would have been completely impossible.

In our complex and ever-changing world, I've learned that every person has the power to affect the thinking and actions of others by what they say and do. It's a multiplying effect which seems to travel far beyond what we normally think is possible. Sometimes just the simplest things said, or actions taken, can have a profound effect on those around us. We never really know the full influence and potential we possess.

Here's a simple question for you to consider. Do you feel your personal existence has changed the world or at least changed specific individuals with which you've interacted? If so, to what degree? If you truly feel your life and its influence has had that kind of power, you're probably better off by having come to that realization.

In conclusion, let me add that I find early each morning to be a valuable time for inner reflection, allowing my life to be more closely examined before starting the day. For me, I refer to those thoughts as 'mind games.' They vary from day to day, but usually end by leaving me refreshed and ready to face the world with a more positive outlook. Hopefully, you also experience some of those same feelings, as you evaluate your own life shortly after waking.

What's It All About, Alfie?

This morning, I received the unwelcome news my ex-father-in-law is in bad shape physically and will probably die in the next few days. He's now ninety-five-years-old and has lived a long, active life up until this last year. As the many events from our fifty-eight-year relationship run through my mind, it's hard for me to keep from wondering, "What's it all about?" With that question, I'm asking myself something specific about life in general. I'm hypothetically thinking beyond his personal situation and considering the entire cycle of life. It's the kind of mental gymnastics I get caught up in almost every time someone I've known for a long time is either about to die or has just passed.

That famous line, in the form of a question, came directly from a song which many of us remember being popular during 1966. Within the first stanza, there's a second thought-provoking question that's worth consideration. It reads, "Is it just for the moment we live?"

In reality, most quality moments experienced throughout our lives are easily passed over, while we get hung up on worrying about either the distant past or the soon-to-occur future. To truly be able to 'live in the moment' is a rare attribute that's easy to talk about, but hard to incorporate into a real part of our daily lives. I've concluded that not many individuals are able to effectively 'live in the moment.'

Time seems to pass quickly, especially the older we get. Most everyone over the age of sixty is aware of that fact. Shortly after we get out of bed in the morning and eat breakfast, it's time again to eat supper. Our days come and go without slowing down, much like grains of sand passing through an hourglass.

The continuous flow of them, one after the other, is accompanied by the knowledge that there's only a limited number still left to experience.

Our overall awareness of the world and its surroundings starts early in life, while we're still very young. At that time, everything is new and different. Gradually, we learn that no one can predict for sure what might happen just around the next bend in the road, either good or bad. With that daily uncertainty to deal with, few of us dwell very long on the thought we'll all eventually grow old and die, unless something else tragic happens beforehand. In our minds, mortality is just not something we need to be overly concerned about until much later. But, before we know it, our lives advance and old age gets nearer, along with possible bad health and regrets that we didn't accomplish all we had earlier planned.

The older I get, the more I seem to spend time mulling over these types of things. A benefit in doing so is that it helps me think through and achieve a better balance of perspective by concentrating to a fuller extent on what's really important.

Another topic worth considering, which falls in the same line of thinking, is 'purpose.' What's my purpose in life? That's an age-old question we've all considered at one time or the other.

Is my purpose in life to achieve something unique, serve my fellow man in a special way, or simply be a decent person who is well respected? Is it to be a good father to my children, a reliable provider for my family, a trustworthy friend to close associates, or just someone who can be counted on by others for help when the chips are down? That list can go on and on and varies for each individual. I think a person's purpose can also change dramatically as the years pass and we progress through life. It's always evolving as time moves forward. What's possible and considered important at a younger age will most likely become a more complex and completely different goal in later years.

To be willing to think it through is valuable in gaining a better understanding of who we are and why we exist. In the process, we can adjust our mental direction, if necessary, to a more beneficial one by fine-tuning meaningful goals and making sure we're on course to advance through our lives with a high degree of focus.

I humbly suggest you give all these thoughts some serious consideration the next time you find yourself alone and thinking about life in general. You might find the time spent in personal reflection to be very useful. I hope that's the case.

For me, I'll continue to hum the song and think about the question it's asking, 'What's it all about, Alfie?' I'm not totally sure what the writer had in mind as he originally put those words on paper, but I know how deeply I've thought about them for most of my lifetime.

A State of Gratitude

There was a time in my life, many years ago, when I struggled mentally and fought daily to keep my head above water and not be pulled down into a severely depressed state. In looking back, I believe my previous expectations had risen to such an unrealistic level I was having trouble feeling satisfied with what life was actually allowing me to experience.

I'd graduated from college ten years earlier thinking I had the world by the tail, requiring only a minimal amount of hard work and effort to make all my wishes come true. What I didn't realize was that I still had a lot more to learn. Life wasn't working out to be as easy as originally planned. When that became most apparent was at the point my health began to be affected because of excess stress. Something had to change, and it had to do with my attitude.

A search was begun to find a creative method in order to deal with my inner frustrations and disappointments. I knew it needed to include altering my present way of thinking, causing a dramatic shift from a more dominant, negative way of viewing things to a positive one. I was convinced there had to be a critical missing element in my thinking which was causing my problems.

Up to that point, I'd often found valuable instruction, knowledge, and encouragement from other people in the form of published books, which covered almost any topic. With that awareness, I immediately drove to a local bookstore where I began my search for just the right one. I was sure there would be a self-help section which contained some very specific information written just for me.

Within one of those volumes, an obvious principle was discovered that had been grossly missing from my consciousness.

It centered around the thought of just how important it was to view everything with a sincere bit of gratitude. No matter how small or seemingly unnecessary, to be inwardly thankful for simple things such as our health, happiness, and family, just to name a few, could lead to a high level of contentment and a more peaceful state of mind. That consideration was part of what I'd been lacking.

The book gave an example of how the author had shown a unique form of his own gratitude to a number of other people, without them knowing who was responsible. The result was a gain for the other individuals, and himself in return. I found what he'd done very interesting.

For one year, he'd decided to anonymously focus on a different person each week who he was sure would benefit from written encouragement. He wanted them to be aware someone cared and felt they were important. The first thing he did was to compile a list of fifty-two individuals. Many of those were people he knew only superficially. He didn't want anybody to suspect he was the one responsible. Research was done to obtain their home addresses. He then purchased some plain stationery, with no name or address.

Every Monday morning, he took about thirty minutes and wrote a personal note that was worded carefully so that each person, one at a time, received a special pat-on-the-back, strong encouragement, and sincere gratitude for who they were and what they were accomplishing within the community. His signature was never added. In the end, he sized up all his efforts as a complete success, in that he felt good after each note was mailed, knowing it would be well received.

After reading about what he'd done and how it made him feel, I decided to do the same thing. Each week I looked forward to picking one of my chosen people from a long list and delivering what I knew would be a welcome surprise with my note of sincere gratitude for their importance and accomplishment in life. Sometimes I'd later pass that person on the street, in a store, or at church assembly and wonder what they'd thought after receiving the short letter. Nothing was ever said about the notes by either me or the people who'd received them.

That exercise gave me such positive feedback, in a secret way, that a decision was made to do something else, which was one step above just sending a note of encouragement and gratitude. After giving it a great amount of thought, I selected ten new individuals. None of whom had been any of the original fifty-two. For some reason or other, I viewed all ten as needing financial help. Once a week, I wrote one of those people a nice note and included a fairly large amount of cash money in the envelope. I handled the wording in such a way that they were instructed to use the money in any way they wanted, as a celebration for who they were as a person. They were told to either spend it or pass it on to another worthy friend. I believe that handling went well, and the encouragement was accepted in the way I intended.

Somewhere along the line, and while I was in the process of accomplishing the above tasks for others, my attitude shifted completely. I became a more positive person who was truly appreciative and thankful for what had been achieved during my lifetime. My stress level noticeably decreased. Upon waking each morning, my main focus was on the many things for which I was grateful, and no longer centered around problems. I was back to being the person I'd always wanted to be. To this day, I still benefit from those actions taken more than forty years ago.

Even though most communication is now accomplished by using the Internet, there's something uniquely valuable to be gained by handwriting a personal note of gratitude, addressing and placing a stamp on the envelope, and then putting it in the mail the old-fashioned way. I encourage you to make this happen with one of your 'special people' in the near future. You'll both come away with a good feeling about what you've done.

The Gift of Laughter

There is something special in being able to look at yourself, your problems, and life in general, and find some humor in it all when faced with a crisis. In most cases, it's easy to take things that happen too seriously.

In making life what you want it to be, I've found that understanding the importance of laughter is a critical step in the right direction. A healthy sense of humor should include an occasional belly laugh that can quickly release excess stress and anxiety from the body and mind. It's a true gift to be able to see the lighter side of life, even in the middle of a very bad situation. Many times, those around us don't see it the same way, but to inject a little humor at just the right time can be beneficial in dealing with others.

In saying that, let me give an example from my own life. Many years ago, I was in the middle of a meeting with the owner of a large corporation. My publishing company had just manufactured and delivered a very expensive, custom-made, printed brochure for his business. He'd been looking forward to distributing it nationwide to promote one of his newest products. There was a glaring typographical error that he noticed on the front page of the brochure, which was the reason I was in his office that day. He was holding me fully responsible for it. In reality, he was at least partially responsible. As a rule of thumb, I never began printing a new brochure without first requiring my client to inspect closely a final proof copy and then sign a standard form indicating he was taking full responsibility. By doing so, he was assuring me that everything was correct.

In this situation, he was the individual who'd signed the form.

His company was a longtime customer, as I'd done business with him for at least fifteen years. During each of those years, I'd handled for him the production of millions of dollars of custom manufactured material, involving many different items.

He looked at me from behind his desk with a troubled expression on his face and said, "Ed...I don't want to be financially responsible for this error, even though I gave you my personal sign-off to proceed after looking over your final proof copy. I want you to cover the expense of my error this time."

I didn't know exactly how to handle what he'd just said. Because I was completely stressed, knowing the value of his yearly business and the large cost to my company involved with this particular job, I began to laugh. I just couldn't help myself. That didn't go over very well.

He aggressively responded by asking, "What in the hell are you laughing about?"

I quickly replied, "I'm very, very sorry. Don't worry, I'll take the loss and completely redo this brochure for you at no additional expense. I'll be glad to do that. You've been one of my top customers for many years, and I view you as my friend. That laugh came out spontaneously in order to relieve some of the built-up stress within my body. For some reason that's the way I occasionally react when stress and anxiety completely overwhelm me. I realize this isn't funny. Your continued business and our relationship are most important and the only things that really matter."

What I said instantly put him at ease. He understood. I went on to correct the problem at a cost to my company of over $40,000, but in the end, I retained the account. Being a true gentleman, he later arranged things so I could recoup my loss by allowing me to add extra to other projects, which he spread out over the next year.

Along that same line of thought, I'm sure everyone recalls a regular column which was printed in the popular magazine,

Reader's Digest. Its title was 'Laughter is the Best Medicine.' I firmly believe that column's title contains a true and valuable statement.

Maybe the next time life is on the verge of dragging you down in the dumps, you can inject a bit of humor and find something to laugh about. A person who can laugh in the face of adversity is an individual who possesses a great gift. The fact is, as I've discovered for myself, laughter 'is' the best medicine.

*When it's all over
and I have permanently left the scene,
I would prefer my friends remember me
in a special way.*

*I want them to all know I gave life
my best effort...at least in my own mind,
and that I'm currently looking down
and feeling good about a truly wild-ass journey.*

Ed Hearn

What You Think About the Most
May Determine the Person You Become

When we open our eyes each morning, it's a little like entering a completely new world, because overnight our mind has had an opportunity to rest, reset itself, and become refreshed. At that moment, we have a chance to either pick up our thinking where we left off the night before, or we can decide it's time for a change in direction and attitude. That's individually up to each of us.

The things we focus on and worry about are usually what materialize in real life in spite of all our concerns otherwise. Life is like that. Our reality, which is different for every person, comes from the way we perceive our surroundings.

We've all heard the two sayings, 'Life is what you make it' and 'Think positively...not negatively.' I've given a lot of thought to both of those familiar phrases. Because we have a reasonable amount of control over our minds and our minds determine what's real and what's not, we should be able to easily manipulate our future. Sometimes that's not so easy because we have to deal with powerful inner emotions and the influence of outside occurrences that are constantly changing.

About the time we begin to feel things are manageable and within our grasp, life will usually let us know everything is about to change. What it comes down to is seeking a state of balance within the chaos. There's always a juggling act taking place in our heads. We fundamentally know where we should be mentally, in order to stay in some degree of control, but getting there can sometimes be tough. While learning to resist a constant pull toward the dark side, we have to keep ahead of that negative momentum by focusing as much as possible on positive attributes.

'You are what you think,' is another saying we've all heard for years, but it's actually truer than most individuals realize. Napoleon Hill wrote a famous novel many years ago titled, *Think and Grow Rich,* which talked about the power of the mind and its ability to control our destiny. It's a book filled with wisdom. I read it around forty years ago and have used many of its insightful concepts throughout my lifetime. All of them are based on common sense and logic. The book is not only about how to attain more wealth, as you might think, but includes numerous ways to ensure you'll live a happy and mentally healthy life. If you've never read it, or haven't re-read it recently, it may be worth your time to do so in the near future.

Another popular saying that was written by W. Clement Stone, a famous philosopher, states 'Whatever the mind can perceive and believe…it can achieve.' That's a powerful statement. It falls in the same category as those other sayings talked about above. They all point out the importance of how we can use and focus our thoughts.

Part of the secret of understanding those principles has to do with our personal awareness. If we know where we want to go in life, and center our minds on a particular outcome, there is a strong chance we can achieve that goal.

Each time we get closer, we gain valuable encouragement. To be aware of what's happening and how we're progressing along the way are necessary elements.

Of great importance, and the main thought to keep in mind, is that your brain is a powerful force. How you use it can control your destiny and create your own reality. Remember that what you focus on regularly and think about most of the time, can easily determine the person you become.

Disinformation

In our current world, there seems to be almost nothing broadcast on the television news, written by editorial reporters in the newspaper, or even publicized on the Internet that can be counted on as really truthful information. The United States has become a country separated by a great divide which is split evenly down the middle as far as our philosophies and lifestyles. One side of that equation seems to rely mostly on their feelings, and how things affect them personally, in deciding what to believe and how to react to it. The other side seems to try and evaluate what's presented to them by using some degree of logic and common sense.

I personally think the best way to mentally sort through the multitude of information we're daily presented would be to combine those two extremes and hit some middle ground in assessing everything. That doesn't seem to be possible in our country any longer.

Nowadays, it only takes less than a minute, while watching any given television news show, to determine which side of the political spectrum is being represented. What it all comes down to is politics. Without hesitation, a talking head will present his or her version of what they feel is correct, and it's obvious they really believe what's being said. There will be backup experts that are interviewed who quickly offer those same insights and beliefs, convinced they are authorities on the subject matter being discussed. By channel surfing, it's easy to get another opposing viewpoint on a different channel; a completely different version given of the same idea, person, or event, and backed up by its own set of professional scholars.

Sometimes it makes my head spin to sit and listen to the insanity presented by mature and apparently educated people. What all of it does tell me, is that I need to always listen carefully to whatever's being said and constantly keep in mind that most of the news outlets are biased in one direction or the other. I need to be responsible for what I choose to absorb and how it's processed in my own mind. It's the same thing when watching the television commercials shown throughout each program that are paying for the airtime, using my own mental skills in evaluating their content is necessary. Just listening to others and believing without a serious, personal critique is foolish on my part.

Local newspapers can also easily present a distorted view in their editorial content which normally focuses strongly to one side, requiring the reader to make a host of intelligent decisions whether to believe or disbelieve what has been printed and distributed on a daily basis. Because of the warped way all of us now receive our information from varying devices, newsprint, and magazines, we need to remain skeptical.

That definitely includes the use of the Internet. I can go nowhere these days where I look around and don't see almost everyone with their heads facing downward, completely absorbed with their smartphone or similar device. Those handheld computers fascinate and rule the majority of people's thinking and lives. It's sad in a way because we were originally promised that the Internet's advanced technology would bring us a better way of life; that we'd have quick availability to communication with our friends, that we'd have the ability to research subjects of interest, and that we'd instantly be able to get the news and weather. I'm not sure, but the whole concept and mechanics may be causing us to move backward. In my opinion, humans seem to no longer be able to think for themselves. They now tend to believe what they see and hear without much serious questioning.

If I sound disillusioned about the whole thing and the direction in which our society seems to be currently moving, you've read me correctly. When whoever out there first started using the word, 'Disinformation,' in reference to the flood of unreliable news from all sources, they certainly went right to the crux of the problem. 'Fake News' is another of those trendy sayings currently in favor that falls in the same category. Both have moved into our lives through the biased media, and I'm talking equally about each side. The problem is they seem as if they're here to stay.

Beginning My Second Life

Shortly after my retirement and move to Wilmington, North Carolina in 1999, I developed a friendship with an older fellow who loved to play tennis, fish, and create artistic sculpture like me. His name was Ray. When we first met, he'd been living the good life of complete freedom from work for roughly five years. He'd moved to Wilmington shortly after retiring from a long career with a large manufacturing business in the northeast. We quickly became good friends due to us both having similar interests in a few common activities.

While on the tennis courts one morning, Ray began to ask me about my past.

He started the conversation between games by saying, "Ed, I'm curious to know what you did for a living prior to moving here. You told me a few days ago that you're from the middle part of Tennessee and recently retired, but I don't know much more."

Being in a talkative mood, I openly began to relay to him some of my work history.

"Ray, I worked in the printing industry as part-owner of a company for over thirty years and am proud of that fact. That job started during the summertime in the middle 1960s, just before I began attending college in another town. When my first college school year began, I enrolled with a full load of subjects and at the same time continued to work three days each week at that printing business located eighty miles away, on Tuesdays, Thursdays and Saturdays. That continuing schedule made all four years of college very difficult, but the eventual degree earned in Business Management was well worth the effort.

During my career, that company grew in size from a very small manufacturing company to a much larger one where I was able to make a nice income for myself and my family. Originally, we didn't own any real estate, operated very old and outdated production equipment, and had very little operating capital. That slowly changed as time rolled by. Each year we reinvested some of our profits and purchased newer and better equipment, while hiring additional skilled individuals to operate the machinery. That trend continued year after year until we were finally known as one of the better organizations of our type in the city. Those aggressive actions helped make us increasingly competitive, so that we could regularly compete with much larger and better financed companies."

"That sounds intense, Ed. The company I worked for most of my career was so large I saw myself as just a cog in the wheel, as they say. Each day I did the same thing, slowly moved up the ladder, and eventually was able to retire. Many of those years, I was bored to death and hated to get up in the morning and go to work. Somewhere near the last five years of my working life, my wife and I began to have troubles. It ended with us getting a divorce. After that occurred, I let it all go and just moved on. I'm now remarried, playing tennis as often as possible, fishing when the weather permits, and creating wood sculptures for fun."

"That sounds very much like my own life. I'm recently divorced after thirty years of marriage and currently trying to readjust to living in a new area of the country, while not having to go to a job each day. The decision to move to Wilmington had a lot to do with its closeness to the ocean. My lifelong love of fishing, the beaches, and the laid-back lifestyle in this town is what attracted me. After only one visit here to check it out, I was hooked."

"Why don't we go fishing together in the near future. I've learned a lot about how to correctly fish from the shoreline, as instructed by some of the old-timers, using bait fish caught in a throw net. The cost is minimal. I can teach you some of what I know, if you'd like to learn. I'm assuming you've mostly fished inland where everything is done differently."

"That's correct. I'd love to go saltwater fishing with you. There's no question it's quite different from fishing in a fresh-water lake. The quicker I can learn your skills, the sooner I can enjoy ocean fishing."

"How about us going tomorrow morning? Would you mind driving to Oak Island near Southport where we can fish around daybreak for flounder and bluefish?"

"That'd be fun. Yes…I'll be glad to do that with you.'

"Let's meet at the entrance to St. James Place Plantation at six o'clock. From there we can transfer everything into my SUV and then drive to the beach. I've got a special spot where I've fished before that will work great. I'll teach you how to throw one of those large, circular nets to catch finger-mullet for bait, and we'll catch a lot of fish. The baitfish swim in large schools up and down the shoreline early in the morning."

"See ya there."

The next morning, shortly after daylight, I was waiting at the entrance to his development as he pulled up. He waved and indi-cated I should move my car to a small parking lot to one side. There, we transferred all my fishing gear to his vehicle. With smiles on both our faces, we were off to the beach for a morning of fun.

Once we arrived, our arms were filled with heavy-duty rods, two tackle boxes, a throwing net, an empty five-gallon bucket, and a cooler full of iced drinks. With that load in hand, mak-ing our way through the loose sand was rather difficult, until we arrived at the water's edge where the sand was packed and much firmer.

"Ed," Ray said. "Get me that net so I can show you the correct way to get it to open fully when thrown. It's an important skill to master. Look out there at all the small bait fish swimming in large schools down the shoreline. You want to toss the net over them. As it quickly sinks to the bottom, the fish won't be able to get out. We can then pull the net's attached cord and empty its contents into this large bucket with water. They'll stay alive as long as we keep a cover over them to shield the sun's heat."

Over the next ten minutes, Ray proceeded to teach me all I needed to know about how to correctly throw the twelve-foot in diameter net. At first it was not easy, but after four attempts, I began to get it to open fully. Before long, we had captured around thirty finger mullet bait fish approximately three to four inches in length.

"Ray, I believe I've got the hang of it. There's definitely a trick to how it's held and how its thrown high allowing time for it to completely open in a wide circle."

Two of those small fish were soon hooked onto the lines of our fishing rods. The baited hooks were tossed into the surf, along with sufficient attached lead weights, to keep the lines in place on the bottom with the strong water currents.

Without much of a delay, Ray exclaimed, "I believe I got a big one trying to take my bait! The way it's biting feels like a big flounder. That particular fish tends to bump the bait slowly before taking it fully in his mouth. When you feel a continued bump on the line, count to ten, and then yank the rod backward to set the hook."

Just as he got those words out of his mouth, Ray jerked the rod upward and back. I watched as his pole bent with a long, continuous arch from the stress and pull of the fighting fish. It swam from side to side, pulling fiercely. Finally, it tired and Ray was able to reel the fish through a turbulent surf and pull it up on the hard sand. We both stared at what he called a 'doormat' flounder. It must have weighed five pounds, with thick flesh on each of its sides.

Once the flounder was placed in our cooler, Ray began asking me more questions about my life before moving to Wilmington.

The first one out of his mouth was, "Ed, I know you told me the last time we were together that you were divorced after having been married for thirty years. How do you now feel about that decision and its abrupt change in your life?"

When Ray asked that question, I assumed he really wanted to know some of the intimate facts relating to my previous marriage, because he'd previously told me just a bit about his own divorce the last time we'd been together.

I began by saying, "It was discovered in a round-about way that my wife had been engaged in a three-year affair with another man. All that took place while I was busy at work. Once all of the details were exposed, I had a rough time getting over the shock."

I then went on to give him even more details, thinking he was interested.

He suddenly stopped me and said, "Maybe I asked that question just a little too directly. You're now giving me more than I wanted to know. I realize the hurt you've experienced is great, it was the same for me. Let me give you some advice I learned a couple of years ago from a very smart friend that will help you cope."

Here's what Ray said to me, and I'll never forget it.

"Think about how good your situation is at this time. Your wife actually did you a favor, even though she doesn't realize it. By her actions, you found out how she really felt, and that ended up setting you free. You're still a young man at fifty years of age. All of that happened in the past. There's no going back. Consider that part of your existence as 'your first life.' You're now living 'your second life.' You can do whatever you want from here on out without being concerned about the past. You've got a lot of living yet to experience. Make the best of it each day and stay positive. Before you know it, your second life will take over your emotions to the point you'll be able to release your hurt and go forward. I can assure you that mindset works. I'm living proof."

"Wow! What an interesting way to view the whole thing. I would have never thought about it in those exact terms. You've made it so simple. From now on, that's the way I'll start thinking."

That conversation took place a long time ago, and I've thought many times about the wisdom Ray gave me that day. He was right. There was no going back; the past was the past. Before my divorce was, in fact, 'my first life.' What I needed at the time was to begin thinking differently. I needed to accept and move forward into 'my second life.' Ray's enlightening insights helped me get there.

If you ever face a similar heartbreak, think about the principle of letting go of the past by separating the past from the present. Once you mentally place yourself in your 'second life,' you'll settle down and create a unique and special world you never knew could exist.

Are 'They' Really Out There?

As I stood looking over my big brother's shoulder, I could see that he was completely focused on flipping through the pages of a strange soft-cover book. The front was sky-blue and approximately five inches wide, eight inches tall, and three-quarters of an inch thick. He guarded that book every time a new one was shipped to our house and would only share some of what it contained if I begged. His newest copy had just arrived in the mail that day.

"I see you've got another one, Bubba. How 'bout you read to me some of the latest sightings? Some of the stuff you shared from last month scared me pretty bad, but I did find it very interesting. Do you really think there's a bunch of aliens visiting our planet?"

"You're full of questions, little brother. Let me scan through the first chapter or two, and I'll find something you might enjoy hearing. As I've told you in the past, the United States Air Force prints and distributes this information and ships the book free to anyone who requests it. My name and address were originally added to their mailing list about a year ago, and I can hardly wait to receive my latest copy near the beginning of each month."

"Yeah…every time you get a new one, your nose is buried in it for days at a time. I can't even get you to go outside and pitch baseball to me until you've finished reading it."

The year was 1958, and it was right in the middle of a hot summer, near the end of July. The publication I'm referring to was named *Project Blue Book*. That was the code name for the systematic study of Unidentified Flying Objects by the United States Air Force from March 1952 until its termination on

December 17ᵗʰ, 1969. Headquartered at Wright-Patterson Air Force Base in Ohio, the project was originally directed by a man named Edward J. Ruppelt. During his tour of duty, and in regard to this study, there were 12,618 UFO sightings in this country, of which many were ultimately ruled as simple atmospheric phenomena or at least explainable to some degree.

I had just turned nine years old, and my older brother was thirteen. To think that there might be 'little green men' running around after landing on earth in flying saucers was almost too much to imagine, but the book included various eyewitness accounts indicating that quite a number of people had actually seen them. Some told stories that they'd been abducted and taken into a spacecraft where physical tests had been administered on their bodies while they were only half awake. Many of those people were later released with a mental loss of time which couldn't be accounted for.

Every week, my brother and I made a point of watching two different shows on television that pushed our imaginations to the maximum about UFOs and other strangeness. One of those was named *The Outer Limits* and the other was Rod Sterling's, *The Twilight Zone.* Both weekly presentations would usually offer subject matter which made our minds question what was really 'real.' They were presented in such a way that the ending of each telecast came across with an almost religious overtone. Or… that's the way I always viewed it. The final few minutes of each show usually contained a moral of some sort, leaving society to question the way we live our lives. Maybe that wasn't obvious to everyone, but for me, that's the way I understood it.

Back in the 50s, a UFO was an 'unidentified flying object.' That mostly included flying saucer-shaped objects or anything out of the norm that was noticed in the sky, either during the day or night. Nowadays, they are referred to as UAPs, which stands for 'unidentified anomalous phenomena.' Both names basically mean the same thing, with a modern-day UAP, which is a catch-all term, describing any unknown object that is detected in the air, sea, or outer space and defies easy explanation.

There's now a very interesting series shown regularly on the History Channel named *Ancient Aliens*. It's well-done with lots of colorful computer graphics and conversation to hold a viewer's attention.

Lately, there's been a lot of conversation about the sighting of intensely lighted orbs, which seem to be showing up all over the world. Many times they can only be seen while using special night-vision, military-type goggles. They can move through the night skies at hypersonic speed, stop, and change direction almost instantaneously, and suddenly disappear as if they're entering a wormhole in space. All of that can be very alarming for an uninformed viewer.

As it turns out, the military has been ignoring the problem for many years, even though they've been aware of their existence. Both military and general aviation pilots have sighted a large number of those objects but have been afraid to talk about them, due to the fact the pilots might lose their jobs if caught publicly talking about it. That part of the phenomenon doesn't really make any logical sense, but it's the way our government has chosen to handle the situation.

At this time, even Congress has gotten involved, trying to eliminate some of the secrecy connected with UAPs. There's recently been special committee meetings, just in the last year or two, about the subject and how those strange objects might affect our country's security.

Take some time tonight and go outside. Look up in the sky and see if you can be the next person to spot one of those strange orbs. Who knows…you might be featured on an upcoming television program where you'll have the opportunity to give an account of your experience. Just be sure to tell 'em you saw ET, the extraterrestrial, and he wasn't just calling home, as made famous in the popular movie by that name from 1982.

What's in a Name?

There was a time when my older brother Travis was around fourteen years old and became interested in the origins of our family name. Up until then, I'd never given it much thought. Without the Internet in those days, I'm not really sure where he obtained his detailed information, but somehow, he found a wealth of knowledge about the subject.

Our family's English surname is 'Hearn.' That word seems to be fairly straightforward and simple, as to how it's spoken and spelled. But, following the extensive work done by my brother, I've realized last names can in fact be very complicated in how they've evolved over time. I'd always assumed that our last name was of German descent, because my mom had made me aware that our great grandmother, on my father's side of the family, was a full German with the maiden name of Heim. That must have also been the last name of my great grandfather. I figured when that part of the family first immigrated from Europe and arrived in America at Ellis Island, the officials there had altered the spelling to Americanize it. I'd been told that was done many times in the late 1800s for families with very unusual last names.

In a conversation I had with a seventy-year-old friend, approximately ten years ago, who had been born and raised in Germany before moving to the United States during the middle part of his life, I asked him about the name. I said to him, "I think my family name originated in Germany. What do you think?"

He stood still for a moment and considered my question before replying, "Ed, I don't believe Hearn is a German name. I think it's either Scottish or Irish."

That took me by complete surprise. I then gave him the additional information about my grandmother and her maiden name.

He replied, "I still don't think it's from Germany, but I understand why you're thinking it is."

After that, I had wondered even more about the name's origin, until yesterday when I stumbled onto some highly detailed information that's been in my possession for over twenty years, but never examined closely. In sorting through a few old storage boxes, a document was uncovered that my older brother had given me sometime in the distant past. Apparently, I'd not been interested in it and just filed it away. For the first time, I read that document carefully. At the top, in large bold lettering, was the name Hearn. Below that heading was extensive wording which answered a lot of the questions I'd pondered over the years.

Let me include here what was stated as part of that document:

"The English surname of Hearn was most likely borne in Ireland by descendants of English settlers by that same name. Their forefathers adopted this English surname as an anglicized form of the Irish O'hEachthigheirn or O'hEachthighearna, more widely seen in Ireland as Ahearne or Aherne. Hearn is the form widely favored in Waterford County, where it is still well represented. Ireland was one of the earliest countries to evolve a system of hereditary surnames. They came into being generally in the 11th century, and indeed some were formed before the year 1000.

In England, Hearn was a local name, meaning 'the dweller at the Herne,' referring to residence in a nook or corner. Local names usually denoted where a man owned his land. Early records of the name mention 'Henry en le Hurne,' who lived in the County of Bedfordshire during 1273. A man by the name of 'Thomas in the Hurne' was listed in the Yorkshire Poll Tax of 1379. There was also a man found in the records named William Crossland, who married Mary Hurne at St. George's, Hanover Square, London in 1773.

The name is also spelled as Hearne, Hurn, Hurne, and Herne.

When the sparsely settled Irish population began to increase, it became necessary to broaden their base of personal identification by moving from single names to a more definite nomenclature. The prefix 'Mac' was given to the father's Christian name, or 'O' to that of a grandfather or an even earlier ancestor.

A notable member by that same name was Samuel Hearne (1745-1792), the English explorer of northern Canada, who was born in London. He served in the Royal Navy, and then joined the Hudson Bay Company, which sent him to Canada's Fort Prince of Wales in 1769. During a journey in search of copper in 1770, he became the first European to travel overland by canoe and sled to the Arctic Ocean. In 1774, he set up the first interior trading post for the company at the Cumberland House, and then became governor of Fort Prince of Wales, where he was later captured and taken to France in 1782. There, his release was negotiated on condition he publish an account of his extensive travels in the New World.

Originally, the official Coat of Arms given a particular family name was a practical matter which served a function on the battlefield and in tournaments. With a helmet covering the warrior's face and armor encasing the knight from head to foot, the only means of identification for his followers was the insignia painted on the shield and embroidered on his surcoat, which was the draped and flowing garment worn over the armor."

After reading the information given above and thinking back in time, I knew Travis had spent a lot of effort researching this project. Beyond just the family name, he ultimately came across an image of our Family Crest and Coat of Arms. Again, I'm not sure exactly where he found it, but vaguely I remember he obtained a book filled with Family Crests and Coat of Arms' images. While still in his teens, he used that documentation to match up our particular family name. As a result, he transferred our Family Crest, in color, to a sheet of paper that was framed and hung on the wall of our home in the early 1960s.

I have no idea what ever happened to that image. I just remember it being colorful and having a few cranes, a type of bird, shown within the crest that Travis said carried a particular meaning. If I could locate that object now, I'd proudly display it on a wall within my office at home.

Pause occasionally and focus on
your worries in life.
Know there are hidden answers
to all problems
just waiting to be discovered.

With patience and prayer
those concerns will
soon be eliminated.

Ed Hearn

Soul Searching

The older I get, the more self-reflective I become. That's possibly a result of where I find myself at the age of seventy-five, combined with my own unique mental makeup. These days, my inner thoughts tend to constantly drift in a variety of different directions, causing me to think about the world in an unfamiliar way. For example, years ago, I rarely caught myself fixating on my ultimate mortality. I was usually focused on simpler things I could achieve or create during meditative moments each morning, so in the late evening I'd have a positive feeling about what I'd actually accomplished. There was little concern about the overall passage of time.

Now…I catch myself thinking about the world of which I'm a part and wondering what it will be like after I'm gone. What will I ultimately leave to this world, allowing others to know I was ever here? What will be my legacy? Is that important? I can't really decide. The hands on my clock seem to constantly move forward, never slowing down. Actually, those hands seem to move forward faster and faster each day. The months and years just plain zip by.

About the time I think I'm adjusting to the condition of old age and my imminent demise; I realize I've got a long way to go before fully coming to grips with those two concepts.

My mind automatically shifts into high gear and consumes my thoughts with questions whenever I find that a close friend or past acquaintance has just died. The first thing I do is go back in time and relive moments spent with that individual. What was it all about? Did I waste that time with them or was it well spent with what we both gained by our mutual interactions? Is that what life is all about…our relationships with others and what we learn from them?

Does everyone else endlessly search their soul for the purpose of their existence the way I think I do? Do others strive relentlessly for a deeper understanding of life's meaning? After much effort, is anything valuable gained? Questions…Questions… where do they end?

Occasionally I'm accused of rambling when I let my mind take over and my mouth starts to speak from feelings generated down deep inside. I guess we're all guilty of that sometimes. It's not all bad. I find there's no better way to analyze what's bothering me than to either be verbal or write down those troubling thoughts, so they can be sorted out carefully. Without either attempting to communicate with others or talking to myself, I have no workable outlet.

Maybe what we leave behind is our own uniqueness in the form of other's memories. But…do memories last very long? Not really. When I look back and consider my own family, I vaguely remember my grandparents, much less my great grandparents and beyond. Those people lived memorable lives, but who recalls anything specifically that they achieved. Yes…they were necessary, so I'd be here today…but what else? What I wish is that at least a few of my descendants would have taken the time to write down their thoughts, their feelings, and some of the things they had to endure and overcome. It would be fascinating for me to read about them and see the world the way they saw it. But…that didn't happen.

That desire, which never occurred, is the reason I'm now writing my own memoir short stories and carrying them through the complete process of publication. By doing so, I'm able to search my mind and reflect back in time on what I've gone through during my life, and ultimately pass on to future generations both my failures and successes, along with who I think I was as a person.

I encourage each and every one of you who reads this story to take the time to write about your own life. You'll be surprised at the number of people who will be interested. If nothing else, your immediate family will find gratification in what you've done, especially if you carry it all the way through to self-publishing your own manuscript.

Losing Friends

Each time I learn that another of my past friends has died, I have trouble adjusting to the fact they are actually gone.

If they had been sick for a long time, and with that knowledge I had the opportunity to slowly adjust and say 'goodbye,' the loss may be easier to handle. If the death is sudden and not expected, my mind usually reflects differently on that situation and our past relationship.

Over the last few years, as I've entered my seventies, both of those scenarios have occurred with more and more frequency. I find myself becoming sad and even a little depressed with every loss of a close friend or acquaintance. I can't seem to avoid focusing for days on many of our more memorable moments which we spent together.

I eventually begin to wonder what it was all about…our brief friendship. My reflections about those circumstances ultimately center on the thought that everything in life must have a purpose. We've all heard that saying. If so, what was the purpose of my becoming friends and interacting with that particular individual? Was there a specific reason for our closeness in years past?

Life is strange, and apparently we need to accept and be ready to adjust on a regular basis in order to survive. A form of constant uncertainty causes us to be emotionally alert at all times, wondering what could possibly happen next.

What we find is that time changes everything. That's another saying we've all heard and a real truism. Given enough time, our thoughts will usually shift to other concerns and eventually the loss of that particular person will not be our primary focus. If not completely, at least partially.

Once I finally work through the necessary grieving process, I can usually get back to living my life as before. In the end, that's what is most important…I guess.

Looking Back in Time

A few years ago, the next to last individual in my direct ancestry from the generation before me, left this world. It was an aunt, a younger sister of my mom. I was curious to discover her age at death and knew by finding her obituary on the Internet, that information could be located. I found she made it to the ripe old age of ninety-four.

What started as simple fact-checking turned into hours of research. Listed with that death notice were the full names of both her parents, which were my grandfather and grandmother on my mother's side of the family. I'd not known either of those individuals since they died in 1940 and 1942, nearly ten years before my birth.

With their complete names in hand, I was able to then find my grandparents' obituaries. It was a big surprise that the Internet was able to provide me with that information. Within those obituaries, I was able to get their parents' full names. Going back farther in time, using that same process over and over throughout my ancestry, I ended up at the year of 1805. Beyond that, there was no additional information to be gained by using the same technique.

That whole side of my family, including mostly the Sullivans and Tidwells, had lived out their lives on farms in various places scattered around Middle Tennessee.

My mom, whose maiden name was Tidwell, had grown up on a pig farm twenty miles west of Nashville where her parents and five other children raised corn and pigs for slaughter. Her dad operated a moonshine still in the hills nearby with a few of his friends. I've told stories about all of that in a few of my published memoir books. It was interesting information that had been verbally told to me over the years.

Once I successfully tracked my mom's ancestry back to well over two hundred years, I was eager to do the same with my dad. Beginning with his dad's death, which I knew occurred in late December of 1958, I found the full names of both of my great grandparents on his side of the family. By leapfrogging from generation to generation, I was able to take his genealogy back to 1804.

I wrote down all of what I'd located and sent copies to each of my siblings. After my sister, Gail, received those detailed copies, she told me she'd recently attended a family reunion where an older lady in her nineties had compiled an extensive family history, including brothers, sisters, and children of many of our relatives going way back. She gave Gail copies of that information, and Gail sent a copy to me.

Upon receiving it, I checked all the information for accuracy. Outside of the individuals I'd known personally, who were correctly included, I found the names of other people that had died before I was born. Many of those, in the generation directly preceding my mom, had been talked about by my mom in the past, as I'd sat and listened to some of her stories. As far as I could determine, there were no errors included.

What had begun as only the desire to find the age of my aunt at her death, turned into a wealth of knowledge about our family, which I've now passed on in written form to my two children, brother, and sister, for their benefit and future generations.

An Evening on the Beach

While recently sitting alone on a wide beach in the Caribbean that extended for at least a mile in each direction, I lifted a handful of sand and began to think about the large number of particles I was holding. In that single scoop, there must have been thousands of individual granules, all roughly the same size.

My actions caused me to start thinking about a statement read recently in a respected science journal. It stated, "There are more stars and planets in the entire universe than the total number of grains of sand on all the beaches of the earth. Each of those stars have their own orbiting planets, similar to what is found in our own solar system."

For the first time that broad statement took on a more powerful meaning. I thought, *that's a lot of stars and a huge number of planets…actually more than my mind can comprehend.*

How can that be possible? In thinking more deeply about it, I knew those statements must be true, since they have been proven by professional astronomers with powerful telescopes and computers capable of scanning deep into the heavens.

I'm regularly exposed to expansive beaches near my home on the eastern coast of North Carolina. On those beaches, there are obviously trillions and trillions of sand particles. If I multiply those staggering numbers by the bits of sand on all the beaches of our world, I'm instantly humbled.

What it shows is how small we are individually, and as a civilization, in comparison to the known universe with its trillions of galaxies, each containing trillions of stars and planets. That in itself shouldn't downplay the value of each individual, but it requires a degree of rationalization to comprehend and use that information in order to visualize the 'big picture.' The billions of people living on our planet, which revolves around our sun, that's only one tiny speck near the outer edge of the Milky Way Galaxy, are all individually important.

For me, whenever my worries and concerns begin to get a little out of control, my tendency is to bring those thoughts to mind and reflect on where I fall in the whole scheme of things. Those mind games seem to be helpful in pulling me back to a more reasonable state of reality.

The next time you feel a need for a renewed boost in perspective, or more importantly, a clearer assessment of your life, stop by the beach and grab a handful of sand. Think about what I've said. More than likely your immediate problems and concerns will get smaller, and you will be able to go back to living your life with greater contentment. It's all a thing of looking correctly at your own situation, as it falls into the scope of everything surrounding you.

It works for me, and I'm sure it will work for you.

*Upon waking each morning,
my first thoughts center around
how best that day can be used
in being productive.*

*If a new creative project can be started
or possibly completed before the sun sets,
I feel I've accomplished something
really valuable with my time.*

Ed Hearn

It's Five O'clock Somewhere

I frequently find myself searching for what's real in this life. Nothing seems to be constant or the way it appears on the surface. About the time I think I have everything figured out, reality begins to set in. From there, I usually arrive at the conclusion I'm nowhere close to seeing things as they actually are. Life is strange in that way...it's all changing and evolving by the moment. Have you ever viewed your situation in a similar way?

In writing this, while enjoying a couple of stiff drinks of bourbon, my inner consciousness seems to be more open to exploring the subjects I'll briefly touch on here. With that fact revealed, here are a few more questions to ponder. Whose ideas should we believe and whose should we reject when discussing the world in general with a friend or acquaintance? We can't believe everything that's said. Each individual we encounter seems to have their own opinion which varies from person to person. Does that bother you or do you accept whatever is presented as fact and just let go of the rest?

My personal belief is that everyone should include a lot of common sense and logic in their daily decisions, but that overly simplified assumption may fall short of the big picture, which tends to vary according to who we're talking to. Many individuals let their emotions control their lives. Everyone is different. A mix of the two variations is probably best to attain some balance.

I've always viewed myself as an out-of-the-box thinker... one who moves forward, only controlled by the beat of my own drum. What I'm about to say may not have anything to do with that last statement.

Oh, by the way, let me stop and let you know that I'm feeling pretty good right now because of the booze, but I'll continue. Please forgive me for rambling a bit.

There are questions I regularly ask myself and never seem to arrive with a solid answer. Here's some of them. After I die, how long will I be remembered? Probably not very long. We're here for only a moment in the scheme of things and then gone forever. What lasting legacy will I leave from my time spent on earth? Who knows for sure...would be my response. Only in the distant future can that question be accurately accessed. By that time, does it really matter? Maybe not.

I've always felt my existence was important. That's probably a little egotistical, with my ego doing the talking, but that conclusion has to be the same for most of us. We struggle with our daily lives, filled with stresses and problems, only to sometimes be let down and disappointed. At the same time, we never completely give up. In reality, are we all just a short blip in time and of no real concern beyond our own internal thoughts?

If, like me, you really want to explore more of your inner self and ask a few additional questions of this same type, I recommend getting completely wasted and then try to write a meaningful short story while searching for answers, as I've just attempted.

It's been fun...but I think I'll now go lay down for a while. Maybe in the morning I can come up with something that makes more sense.

Getting Old

My dad walked up to me nearly thirty years ago and asked, "Ed, what day is it?"

Without giving his question much thought, I replied, "Dad, it's Saturday."

He stared off in the distance and didn't say anything more for a short while. Then he started up again by saying, "You know, since I retired almost fifteen years ago, I've sort of lost touch with time and the days of the week. No longer do I recognize the difference between the five workdays and the two days of the weekend. They all seem the same to me. When I was employed, I was very aware of which days were workdays, Monday through Friday, and was always glad when the weekend rolled around."

"I can certainly understand what you're saying. In fact, you no longer really need to keep up with the different days. For me, it's still important since I'm still working, but for you, every day is a holiday."

With that said, both of us looked at each other for only a moment and then laughed, as he patted me on the shoulder.

"Yes, son, you're right, but it bothers me a little that I am no longer able to keep up with the individual days as I once did. Without the morning newspaper, that I occasionally read, I'd lose track completely. Actually, I guess I don't really care. Does that make any sense?"

"Dad, you're a lucky man. Look at it this way. You worked hard for forty years in a monotonous, blue-collar job at a large factory. You raised a good family and have been financially responsible for most everything during your entire life. Give yourself a break and just enjoy the freedom. Let us younger people worry about what day it is."

"I guess you're right. How 'bout us going fishing this after-noon?"

"That should be fun. I'll get the rods, bait, and lifejackets and meet you at the boat dock in a few minutes. You go on down and get the boat ready. We'll be out there catching some catfish before you know it."

"Hey…that sounds good. I think I have plenty of gas already in a metal container inside the boat. Did you pick up any earth-worms from the bait shop on your way here?"

"Yep…sure did. Got some of those large nightcrawlers the fish seem to love. We'll start slaying 'em shortly and definitely have a good time."

Within twenty minutes, we had everything on board that was needed and were cruising out of his cove into the main channel of the lake. The whole area was familiar to me because it was where I'd grown up.

Shortly after I'd turned twelve, Dad and Mom bought a piece of land on the edge of a newly formed lake in middle Tennessee. For a year or so afterward, our entire family of six used that location to pitch a tent during many hot summer weekends. It served as a nice getaway for everyone. Together, we'd built a reasonably-sized boat dock where we fished, swam, and docked our small, aluminum boat. We'd regularly build a campfire in the evening and use two gas lanterns to provide light after the sun went down. It was all great fun.

Dad and Mom later built a house on that land. It was small, when compared to others in the area, because our family didn't have a lot of extra money at the time. But, the structure served its purpose.

As Dad and I approached the spot on the lake where we'd caught a number of large catfish in the past, he slowed the boat so I could drop the anchor. Once in position, our hooks were each baited with a large worm before they were cast in the water. Before long, we started getting a few bites.

Suddenly, Dad hooked into a big one. He began to get excited as his rod arched downward and bent almost double. Slowly, the fish was played back and forth until it eventually tired, which allowed me to hoist him into the boat with the aid of a large net.

Once that had been accomplished, I looked over and noticed a big smile on his face. It was obvious he was having a good time.

After catching three more fish and the passing of about an hour, he turned and said to me, "Ed, I'm getting a little tired. We've caught plenty of catfish and can cook one of 'em for supper. I'll release the others. How 'bout we head back to the dock and call it a day?"

"I'm fine with that. I'll get the anchor in the boat, if you'll get the motor started. We'll be at the dock in less than ten minutes."

"That'll be nice. I just get tired too easily these days. I've really enjoyed being out here on the lake with you. If you'll help me clean that big catfish, I'll fry it up in our cast iron skillet for tonight's meal."

"Dad, I can hardly wait."

As I think back to that day, many years ago, I remember my dad as a caring person who always was willing to go out of his way to help his children. He loved to fish, and he loved to spend time with us while doing a variety of activities.

Dad died at the age of seventy-four. That's the same age I've now reached. Time goes by quickly, and before we know it, we all find ourselves older than we think we should be.

I guess that's just the way life goes...

Stress and Anxiety

Have you ever thought about how disruptive both excess stress and anxiety can be in affecting your daily life? For many people, those two things, the first being physical in nature and the other an emotional response, are primary concerns which constantly hinder their productive efforts at home and work. Each morning when the sun comes up, worrying begins about their family, finances, or overall health and picks up right where it left off the night before. There seems to be no way to get away from those concerns or satisfactorily resolve the problems. Day after day, the same issues are always on their minds, usually appearing in negative forms.

To make matters worse, the television is turned on, so its noise will serve as a distraction, but by doing so, the news appears with talking heads going on about all the tragedies which occurred overnight either locally or around the world. Everything surrounding us seems to be in some state of crisis.

Then, one of our handheld electronic devices is picked up to check who has been trying to reach us by email, Twitter, or through a text message. We know they are expecting a quick response to whatever was sent. If our Iphone dings, a rush of adrenalin begins, somewhat similar to what happens when we take a stimulating drug. Strange feelings wash over us. We're instantly keyed up until the message is read and our response is sent. It's a crazy world. Nowadays, almost everyone has one of those devices which was originally marketed as something to make our lives easier. In fact, just the opposite has taken place. They've caused almost everyone to constantly be on an emotional edge. Getting our morning fix of caffeine by consuming an espresso drink or just plain coffee, followed by a little nicotine from a quick cigarette, only adds to that stress and anxiety.

As a society, we no longer relate to each other the way we once did. There's not nearly as much personal interaction or face-to-face contact. That applies to both our children and many of the adults around us. We feel isolated in an odd way. Our children don't go outside and play with neighbors, like we did as kids, they want to play games on those machines. We don't sit down quietly to eat supper and have a pleasant discussion as a family without one of those things interrupting our meal.

Wherever I go, when I look around, nearly everyone is holding an Iphone or another one of those electronic devices with their face stuck in front of the lighted screen. What's happening around them is not of real concern. They're temporarily lost in space, some location similar to the Twilight Zone.

For me, I've tried hard to stay away from that new world insanity which has sprung up all around us. I don't own an Iphone, Ipad, or whatever other mobile device happens to be popular at the time and don't have any desire to have one. I do communicate on my personal computer at home using email, but it's done on my terms. I choose when I want to check my emails and when I want to respond. It gives me time to think through my response and keeps me from becoming overly stressed in the process.

I own a flip phone which is kept in my car for long trips. It stays turned off most of the time. Occasionally, it is given a charge, and then replaced in the car's console until needed on the road sometime in the future. In the process of charging it, maybe once every two or three months, I'm sometimes made aware there's a message. Instinctively, I know it's been there for a while. Because of my electronic quirkiness, I try to let everyone know I seldom answer that phone and rarely give out its number, telling them it's mainly for emergencies. My older son occasionally calls and leaves a message on that cell phone, knowing my strangeness, and will say with a laugh, "Dad...you may not get this message for a few weeks or even a month or two, but I've called just to say hello and check on you. Call me whenever it's convenient. I love you."

I realize my handling is viewed as insane in our current world, but I see it as the best way for me to remain calm each day and enjoy my life. Being retired gives me the opportunity to live in a different manner than most people. Thank the Lord for my current situation. During my working life, I faced more than my share of stress and anxiety. I know how harmful it can be.

These days, I try to chill out most of the time and enjoy the moment. Think about what I've said and join me...if you can.

The Golden Years

Long ago, when my retired parents reached their middle sixties, they both began playing softball one evening a week with a team of older, retired friends. They referred to that period of their lives as 'the golden years.' Both Mom and Dad had available time and were still healthy enough to get out and interact physically with others. They'd laugh, talk, and overall enjoyed visiting with individuals roughly their same age. It was good for them.

I've personally tried to participate in similar physical activities in my own life. After retirement, beginning nearly twenty-five years ago, many days have been spent playing tennis and golf, fishing, and traveling, plus regular involvement in numerous other sports. To be outside in the open air, with sunshine beaming down, always seems to put a smile on my face. In that setting, my attitude always improves, and at the same time new friendships can be easily formed.

While I worked at my everyday job and spent a lot of time indoors at the office, I'd frequently stare out the window next to my desk and wonder what it'd be like to be free to do whatever I wanted with each day. There were customers who told me, upon observing my obviously busy schedule, that there was no way I could ever retire. They didn't think I'd be able to separate myself from the daily grind, which they thought I somehow thrived on. It's common knowledge that some people live and breathe their jobs. It's part of who they are as a person and makes them feel important. Without the job, they don't feel their lives have any real purpose.

I knew that was not me. I dreamed about a time in the distant future when I'd be able to do just about anything I pleased with my days. At least I hoped that time would eventually come. I never saw myself as 'living for the job.' The job was only a way to earn enough money so eventually I could retire and have fun. It wasn't ever viewed as an end-in-itself, as some people tend to view their own jobs.

In looking back, I remember a special day of enlightenment that had a definite long-term effect on the way I viewed the future. It occurred around the time I reached the age of thirty-five, when the realization suddenly hit me that there was a totally different world out there, from the one I experienced each day at the office. In my world up to that point, I'd wake in the morning, drive to work, stay involved with solving problems for everyone until the late evening…and later return home to eat, so that soon afterwards I could go to bed. That insanity was repeated day-after-day, year-after-year, with no apparent change in sight.

On that particular day, which happened to be a Wednesday, there was an important customer coming to the printing business where I worked, to press-check his color brochure while it was running on one of the larger presses. In trying to prepare for his arrival with only an hour to spare, I walked down one of the main aisles between two machine operators, just as one of them was busy adding thick, black ink to his press cylinders using a fully loaded putty knife. As I passed, he turned around, not knowing I was there, and accidentally smeared a glob of it on the front of my brand-new blue shirt.

Instantly, I had a problem. I looked at my watch to confirm I had time to quickly drive to a major department store, located not too far away, so I could purchase a new shirt before my client arrived. That was accomplished…but while walking through the main part of the mall to reach that particular store, a large number of people were observed just milling around. There were lots of women, some of them with their children, but there were also a large number of men…more than I expected. My first thoughts were…*What do these people do for a living? Do they not have jobs like me? How are they able to be here in the mall apparently just killing time, on a Wednesday, during the middle of the day?*

As a result of that observation, I decided there must be another world out there, different from the one I lived in. That was the day I knew that sometime in the near future, I too, would be able to visit the mall during the week, casually walk outside to spend time in the sunshine, engage in any activity of my choosing without hesitation, or anything else I chose to do with my free time without feeling guilty.

Eventually that time came. I retired and have enjoyed fully every day since then. Having been tied to a restricting job for so many years, the comparison of how I live now, with my current freedom versus my old way of existence, is glorious indeed.

The negative tradeoff of having arrived in that new existence is age. To finally get to the point of being able to retire means you're probably an older person. At this time, I'm seventy-four, and only five months from reaching seventy-five. That statement is a little humorous as I write it, because my mom had a habit of frequently jumping to the next year whenever she was asked her age. If she'd just turned eighty for instance, she'd tell anyone who asked her that she was almost eighty-one. I guess I just did the same thing myself. Oh, well…so much for being influenced by others.

Getting back to my story, this morning I talked briefly to a middle-aged friend who's a security guard and was on duty at the time. Our discussion centered around him feeling trapped in his current phase of life where he has to earn a living by holding down a demanding job. During our conversation, he told me that he hoped to someday retire. At that time, he wanted to travel across the entire United States with his brother and play golf in every single state. He told me that up until now, he'd not been able to visit but a handful of other surrounding states throughout his lifetime from the one in which we both lived. I found what he had to say quite interesting, because of the same type of dreams I'd once had concerning retirement.

We all dream. But, we're usually forced to put off our immediate desires to spend time working a job to survive financially. It takes money to live. That's life in a nutshell. I'm just glad circumstances have made it possible for me to enjoy my Golden Years. Hopefully they'll last for a long, long time to come.

One of the More Important Things in Life

Throughout my lifetime, I've interacted with a large number of different people. We all do that as part of daily living. After a period of time, through repeated interaction and commonalities in viewpoint and interests, some of them naturally became my sincere friends. I've found we tend to make friends with people we cross paths with on a frequent basis. The more we see someone, the more likely a friendship is to develop. It always helps if we share common interests. It's easy to be drawn to someone who is similar to us; with the same hobby, cultural background, career path, or a person whose children are about the same age as ours.

A true friend is valuable and should be cherished, because he or she usually becomes someone we can open our hearts to without fear of criticism or rejection. They can usually be relied on in times of trouble, giving us a way to share our innermost thoughts, while in return receiving reliable and common-sense advice. At the very least, they can serve as faithful companions who will join us in everyday activities; things as simple as joining us for lunch or spending time watching a movie at the cinema.

General characteristics of a good friend normally include someone who shows a genuine interest in what's going on in our life at any given time. They are usually interested in what we have to say about things which are somewhat private in nature, and also interested in how we inwardly think and feel about a variety of other issues we won't freely share with the general public. They freely accept us for who we are. A good friend will listen carefully without making judgments and openly share private matters about themselves.

A strong friendship always works both ways. It should be an interaction between two individuals where both people feel comfortable supporting and accepting, and at the same time enjoying a bond of complete trust and loyalty.

Having a good friend tends to bring more happiness into our lives than almost anything else. That relationship can have a huge impact on our mental and physical stability. With healthy back-and-forth verbal interaction, we can relieve stress, provide for a greater sense of our personal well-being, and prevent excess loneliness or isolation.

It's never too late to make new friends and reconnect with old ones. Some of the immediate benefits can be an improvement in our moods, an energization toward achieving new goals, reduction of depression as we age, and an overall boost to our self-worth.

Having friendships online is not the same as having a close friend to spend time with in person. Our most important and powerful connections occur when we're face-to-face. If a friendship feels good, usually it is good. But if a person tries to control you, criticizes you, abuses your generosity, or brings unwanted drama or negative influences into your life, it's time to re-evaluate the friendship.

As the years have rolled by, some of my past friends have gradually fallen by the wayside. Occasionally one or two of them have been lost because of their untimely deaths, which were definitely tragic events for both me and their families. In other instances, a few have moved to other parts of the country due to a job change or other personal issues creating a huge distance gap and resulting in us not being able to see each other as often as before. Those who have remained friends for as long as twenty, thirty, or even forty years are truly part of life's treasures.

Why not pick up the phone and give an old friend a call today? He or she will appreciate it, and you'll both feel better for your efforts. Be sure to tell them how much they've meant to you over the years. I'll bet they'll return those same feelings. We all need friends, and good ones are hard to find.

*Whatever life stresses are currently
weighing you down,
have faith and believe things will
soon get better.*

*Try to relax and enjoy each moment
to the fullest.
This is your time to shine.*

Ed Hearn

Acts of Courage

This morning, I began to think about courage and what it takes to be courageous. It's a bigger deal than most of us realize. Over my lifetime, I've not given either of those terms much thought until now.

Let me begin with a crude attempt to define the word 'courage.' In my opinion, a person displays that honorable trait whenever he or she spontaneously pushes beyond their comfort zone, without concern for themselves, to achieve a dangerous goal that was previously unexpected. Many times, that act occurs with very little advance consideration of possible personal agony, pain, danger, or intended consequences. The hope is that a favorable outcome will occur and later be viewed as either a highly respected accomplishment or as a positive, major life-changing event.

To carry the definition a bit further, let me quote directly from the Internet and Wikipedia with a short definition of 'courageous.' It states, "to be courageous, a person should possess the quality of being ready and willing to face negative situations including danger or pain, without fear, but it can also involve facing those same conditions despite fear."

Many years ago, I was forced to make a quick decision involving life or death. I mean 'quick' because my response to the specific event was initiated by a sudden rush of adrenaline, and not as a result of my having taken the time to evaluate the crisis prior to putting myself in harm's way. Maybe my actions could currently be considered courageous, but more accurately, I think they should be viewed as having lacked sufficient pre-planning prior to my response to a serious emergency.

That story has already been told in one of my earlier memoir books about my efforts to save my very young sister's life when she fell out of the boat in which only the two of us were riding, while neither of us were wearing a life jacket. She couldn't swim, and I foolishly dove in without first picking up and taking a life preserver with me. Since we were both fully clothed and I was wearing tightly laced shoes, I became physically exhausted more easily than expected in an attempt to drag her to the shallow water.

Without the aid of our father, who watched from the shoreline what was happening and who jumped into another powerboat moored nearby to get us, we both could have easily drowned. Looking back, my efforts could be considered courageous because of an emotional adrenalin rush, but the facts are I didn't use much common sense in handling that emergency. If I'd carried a flotation device into the water with me, all the danger would have been eliminated.

In searching my memory for other outstanding acts of personal courage, I have trouble coming up with more than a few insignificant incidents I could write about. In retrospect, most of those seem somewhat minor in comparison to stories I've heard involving real heroes throughout history. So...what I want to add here is a story about amazing and unusually raw human courage.

The United States, along with British and Canadian troops totaling 152,800 soldiers, stormed fifty miles and five major beaches of Normandy, France on June 6, 1944. It was a massive amphibious invasion of German-occupied France, in western Europe, known as D-Day. The beaches were fiercely defended by the Germans who lined the hillsides occupying mile after mile with heavy fortifications.

I knew a gentleman that died only a few years ago at the age of ninety-eight who was one of those American infantry soldiers. As he described his involvement to me, and the risks that were taken that dreadful morning, there was no question in my mind of his extreme bravery and courage. I could hardly perceive him having been a part of that horrible experience, as he watched many of his comrades fall to his side who had been killed instantly by German machine gunners overlooking the invasion from hillside bunkers nearby.

The United States' involvement included 54,000 infantry troops which suffered 2,700 casualties. The British had roughly 54,000 soldiers and lost 1,030 individuals. The Canadian troops included 21,400 and approximately 1,200 were killed. There were additional Allied Airborne troops totaling 23,400, of which 3,999 were killed by the Germans. Each of those men displayed extreme courage in being part of that operation. Their ultimate goal of taking that beach and freeing France had become more important to them than the loss of their individual lives.

My friend was one of those men. Each time I looked at him, after hearing his story, my heart was filled with respect, gratitude, and awe with what he and others had accomplished. What he'd been involved with was a true Act of Courage, never to be forgotten.

What Should Not Be Forgotten

In thinking back over my life and trying to decide on just one especially powerful memory, what comes to mind is a statement my father made to me near the end of his life, while knowing he was gravely ill with only days left to live.

He solemnly looked up at me as I stood by his bedside and said, "Ed, I'm proud of you and our entire family. The closeness shared between us has made it all worth my efforts. Even though I'm not completely ready to go, I'm aware my work on earth is done. I want to leave you with a brief message of encouragement.

Don't ever give up, no matter what life presents for you to endure. Face every day with hope and a sense of humor. Live in the present, because that's all you can control. Above all, know I love you. Always be kind to yourself."

I've written other stories in my various memoir books about my father. He was a kind and generous man who I greatly admired. To lose him so early in life to congestive heart failure, at the age of 74, was a complete shock for me. What he left behind was a wonderful legacy, giving me direction in how to live my life successfully. His example was powerful and influenced the way I now approach each day.

Even though he didn't have a lot of money, he worked hard and was honest with his feelings and sincere in the way he treated others. I could always count on him to help me when I expressed a need. That wasn't very often, because I respected his time and energy, but he was there for me and our family, over and over, at critical times.

At this moment, I'm older than my dad was when he died, by almost a year. That seems very strange, because I don't necessarily feel very old at 75. Time does go by quickly. His advice about 'living in the present' was a gift I've not forgotten, and for him to have stated that he loved me was possibly one of the best things he could have said.

I just hope I can be that same type of person to both of my children. Life is not easy. In the end, for them to know they're not alone, and that I care, can be one of the most important things I can offer.

Long live Dad's memory...

Changing of the Seasons

Another year has finally entered its third quarter, and the fall season has arrived. On the east coast, I've found that on many of the days from the last week in June until the middle of September, it can be nearly unbearable outside. Extreme heat and humidity seem to rule, with very little change, until the season shifts in September. During the middle of summer, I usually have a visual image of myself stepping out of a comfortable, air-conditioned home and entering a heated oven, as the hot air seems to be relentless. Along with that condition, there's normally very little breeze circulating to temper the situation.

The short gap of time between those two seasons comes and goes so quickly that the transition is similar to someone flipping a light switch. Within a matter of only a day or two, there's a coolness which develops in the air for the first time since late spring. Suddenly, it's again nice to be in the great outdoors.

A negative aspect of the late summer to fall seasons, in eastern North Carolina, has to do with hurricanes. From the middle of June to early November each year, there are continuous violent storms that move across the Atlantic Ocean, which originate in northern Africa. From satellite imagery, they seem to move westward, in a counterclockwise manner, like large bowling balls, with one chasing after the other. Some of those stay to the south and eventually hit the Yucatan Peninsula of Central America, after passing over Puerto Rico, while others enter the Caribbean and then move north to either Texas, Louisiana, or western Florida.

The ones I fear the most are those that either travel up the eastern coastline or those that directly hit eastern North Carolina. Since I've lived in the Wilmington area for the past twenty-five years, only a couple of miles from the beach, there have been numerous hurricanes that have made landfall in our area. When the weather channel on television shows satellite photos on their sky map that one is headed directly towards us, it's usually given a rating of either Category Two or Category Three. When the rating is stronger than that, it's time to leave town. It's not uncommon for some of the larger hurricanes to span up to five hundred miles across with a much narrower, calm eye in the center.

We've had a few that were rated as either Category Four or Five while still circulating hundreds of miles off the coast, but those seem to dissipate in strength and wind speed as soon as their huge, outer cloud bands start moving across land. That's way before the extremely high winds arrive that are located more to the middle. Those storms can quickly shift down to Category Two or Three, which makes a great deal of difference.

With wind speeds of under one hundred miles an hour or slightly greater, Category One and Category Two hurricanes can still do tremendous damage in a short amount of time. Huge amounts of rainfall are usually dumped in low areas causing dangerous flooding, while at the same time, their violent winds can destroy millions of dollars of value in real estate. Even loss of life is possible, and that frequently occurs.

In North Carolina, we get to experience all four seasons of the year. It's never boring here. I personally prefer either spring or fall. They're both enjoyable and allow for outdoor activities, without either suffering from profuse sweating or the shivering cold.

To round out the changing of seasons, there are three major holidays which take place through the fall and early winter. They give everyone something special to look forward to. There's Halloween at the end of October, Thanksgiving near the end of November, and then Christmas on December 25th. Once that last one has come and gone, spring, with all its beauty, is not far into the future.

Intuition

While in the process of recently composing a fictional short story, I began to think about how my mind actually worked as it formulated various thoughts in connection to developing an entertaining plot. At one point, there was the feeling my story needed a unique twist in order to catch the reader by surprise, hold their complete attention, and ultimately create a unique ending.

I began to receive a few mental possibilities which came to me as clear visions. They seemed to appear from nowhere. Out of the blue…there they were. All I had to do was choose one of them and incorporate it into my writing. As easily as that happened, it made me think, where did those ideas suddenly come from?

After analyzing that question, my conclusion was that I'd drawn from a lifetime of experiences. Using my stored memory, which included a vast number of past events, I'd quickly sorted through a mass of information and arrived with a variety of possible solutions. With very little effort, my inner creativity had taken over.

Once that occurred, I began to consider how the term 'intuition' might have fit into what had just taken place. Curiosity had the best of me, so I went to the Internet and looked up the meaning of that word to get a better understanding.

What I found was this definition, along with some extra thoughts I'll expand on below: "Intuition is an instantaneous understanding or recognition of something, without the conscious use of reasoning or analytical abilities. It can manifest as a sudden inkling, an instinctive reaction, or a 'gut feeling' about a particular situation or decision."

Now, that's pretty heavy stuff, I thought.

I believe that in my case, while writing a fictional story, once my mind offered a few possible solutions for different directions I could take for the best result, that's when natural intuition stepped in. As strange as it seems, a gut feeling for the best course of action materialized.

Intuition, in many forms, may very well come into play in a large variety of ways throughout our lives. For example, when we're attempting to understand something, without taking the time for conscious analysis in advance, we might conclude to just "allow our intuition to guide us." It's a little like being 'on autopilot' to help us make unconscious decisions which we can rely on.

Have you ever been in a bookstore and felt drawn to a particular book for an unknown reason, only to later discover it offered you some special insight that worked to be beneficial in your life? I've done that, and it's a little strange when looking back in reflection.

Have you ever been driving down a busy roadway in the left-side lane of traffic that's all traveling in the same direction and decided to change to the right-side lane, only to observe a car traveling in the opposite direction uncontrollably swerve into your previous lane of traffic? Maybe that's a little of the thing called intuition at work.

Throughout our lives, we're affected by our intuition in more ways than we realize. Never more than when we're faced with making a major decision. An example of that situation would be whether to accept a new job or remain in the same one we've had for years, after a promising opportunity has just presented itself. That's a time for the special gift of intuition to come into play. We have to make a decision which will affect not only ourselves, but our entire family. What we do depends somewhat on our intuition. Good or bad…we've got to decide.

However it's looked at, there's a host of reasons all of those different ideas popped into my head, as I searched for a particular direction in which to take my fictional story. The good part was that I chose one of those scenarios which seemed to fit perfectly. The unique twist it added was just what the doctor ordered. Be it intuition or just plain off-the-wall creativity, in the end, the final story somehow worked out to be a good one. I guess that's all that really matters.

When you look back over your life,
do so with great respect for what has been accomplished.
Realize there are varying levels of achievement.
Be proud.

Not everyone may view it the same way.
For you...be content and at peace with yourself.
God will be the one who makes the final decision.

Ed Hearn

What's Really Real...If Anything?

Reality is merely an illusion, albeit a very persistent one, of which that illusion of reality normally tends to shift over time.
–Albert Einstein

When I was an inquisitive kid of fifteen years old, I can remember having an interesting conversation with my mom one day after I asked her, "Mom, in your opinion, what's really real and what is not real in the world in which we live? This is something I've been thinking about for a while, and I'd like your thoughts."

To me, it sounded as if my question should have been an easy one to answer, but she hesitated in giving me a response and just listened as I continued talking.

I'd been studying a list of questions and concepts that I'd recently read, which had my mind churning. Here's a few of those:

1. Can we ever be sure that our personal perception of things is right? Is the act of consulting others a good way to determine this?
2. How do we differentiate between good and bad, when in reality it all depends on our perspective?
3. Is the reality of the world different from how we perceive and experience it in our minds?
4. Does physical reality exist apart from the human mind?
5. Is there anything that is actually real, since there are theories suggesting that everything we know could be imaginary.

This will give you a bit of my thought process which caused me to get into the conversation with her.

Our discussion got a little complicated when she asked me, in return, a simple question. "Why do you care what is actually real and what is not. Does that really matter?"

I told her, "If it bothers me to not know the truth, that's all that needs to be considered. My personal view of a particular situation should be the determining factor." In an effort to add a bit more explanation, I said, "Without me and my personal feelings in the equation, I feel none of this world which surrounds me is really important. Whatever is fixed in my mind as an individual perception of myself should rule over everything. I believe I'm the one who actually determines what it real and what's not."

I was trying to tell her that I felt strongly about how others felt and perceived the world. I cared about their perception. She had other feelings and saw things from a different viewpoint.

Mom had an aggressive type of personality and was a person with strong thoughts about life in general. She'd grown up on a rural farm with many brothers and sisters who all performed numerous chores each day. It was a tough life that made her mentally strong and independent with her thoughts and actions. Sometimes she was known as a little hard-headed, because she made a point of not letting others determine how she reacted or allowed them to force their feelings on her without her approval.

The more we talked, the more convinced she was that she was right. In her opinion, I should not be worried about what anyone else thought, where I was involved. To the same intensity, I was convinced that what others thought was of immense importance. We were at a standstill.

Finally, she realized I wasn't going to change my mind. At the same time, I knew she wasn't going to change hers. As an end result, we agreed to drop the conversation.

Afterwards, I spent some time re-evaluating my thinking, only to come to some of the same conclusions. I couldn't get out of my mind the thought that 'without MY active consciousness in play, none of what seemed to be reality really existed.'

I feel it's that way for everyone. We're all the captain of our own ship. As long as we're alive and functioning, we're creating for ourselves a form of reality. Once we die, that reality no longer exists. We come into this world and are surrounded by an instant consciousness that only we create. We leave this world at death and take nothing with us. We're completely gone at that time and our personal reality leaves with us.

I know this all sounds strange but think for just a moment about those people who were close friends in your life, that are gone due to death. Where is their reality now? Did it really ever exist? We're here by ourselves surrounded by our own form of reality. It's completely different for everyone.

What I'm saying is totally counter to most of what we're taught and think about in regard to our lives and reality in general. I know that.

These are some of the type things I think about when I have idle time to sit and reflect. Sometimes it gets a little crazy, but that's okay. What's really real...if anything... is worth giving some extra thought...when you have the time.

Would Someone Please Stop Ringing That Bell?

Beginning in 1959, I lived for eight years in a small apartment with my entire family at a special school in Nashville, Tennessee. That apartment was located within a large, two-story structure where my mom worked as a dormitory supervisor in charge of around sixty male students. Those who had been assigned to her dorm varied in age from thirteen to seventeen. Most of those housed in her building attended either the ninth or tenth grade. Mom's job required her to be responsible for everyone seven days a week, twenty-four hours a day.

In total, there were approximately seven hundred children, both male and female, who were a part of that school, which offered classes all the way from the first to the twelfth grade. In addition to the children, there were around one hundred and fifty staff members, including other dorm supervisors, administrative personnel, teachers, coaches, cooks, and maintenance employees.

The school was unusual in that the kids lived there year-round. Very few of them ever went home during the school year or during the summers. In general, their earlier home life had caused many of them to be either socially or financially at a disadvantage in one way or the other. Because of a previous, unfavorable home environment, most all of them had been assigned by a judge in the Nashville juvenile court system to be a part of that particular state supported school, so they could grow up and be cared for, while getting a good education.

Now, with that background information out of the way, here's what I wanted to talk about. My mom was the person who controlled the timing throughout each day for most of the major activities. There were so many individuals under her care that she had to use a set of electrically operated bells mounted on the walls, which would ring throughout the building whenever she flipped a control switch. Those bells were timed by her in such a way as to let everyone know they needed to begin certain actions, which had been assigned for particular times. After only a short period of regularly hearing that irritating noise, most everyone learned the meaning of each individual bell without having to be told what it stood for.

Each day started at 6:30, when she flipped a light-switch type controller and rang the first bell of the morning. The noise sounded loud enough throughout the entire structure that no one could possibly miss hearing it. That bell was the signal to get out of bed, get dressed, and make up your bed, so it would pass inspection for neatness.

The next bell, only ten minutes later, indicated that everyone was to begin doing their assigned morning chores throughout the dorm. Each person had been assigned a personal task to complete before he was allowed to eat his first meal of the day. The chores rotated every two weeks, so that eventually each boy performed every different task at least once from month to month.

The entire building had to be cleaned, and that was repeated over and over every morning before breakfast. Those chores included tasks such as mopping the floors in the bathroom stalls, cleaning all the toilets and sinks with a disinfectant solution, buffing the tiled floors with a power buffer after first sweeping those areas, dusting all the furniture, straightening up anything out of order, organizing the numerous chairs and tables, sweeping the outside sidewalks, raking leaves and picking up any debris in the yard, which contained a large number of large maple and hackberry trees.

After about twenty minutes, another bell was rung which indicated everyone needed to quickly brush their teeth and wash their hands. Following that activity, all sixty guys assembled either inside the front hallway during the winter or on the outside sidewalk during the summer months, where roll was called by Mom making sure each student was present and ready to walk together to the main cafeteria for breakfast.

Once we'd all eaten, along with all the other boys from other dorms who had arrived at the same time as us, we returned to our dorm to get ready for that day's school activities, if it was one of the days between Monday and Friday. The girls had their own cafeteria on the far side of the campus where they ate breakfast and supper in a similar way.

It wasn't long before another bell was heard at ten minutes before eight o'clock, which indicated we needed to assemble for one more roll call before disbursing to our classes that were held in the high school building, only a short walk away. Inside that building, the bells didn't stop. When we were in school, the bell rang each hour to change classes, then we had only five minutes to get to our next class. At that time, there would be another bell for that class to begin. If you weren't in your seat, you would be considered tardy.

Both males and females ate together for lunch at the same, main cafeteria, during regular school days. We generally walked there along with the entire class we'd just attended before lunchtime.

After school ended at three o'clock, everyone was free to play outside, near their own dorm, for a few hours before supper. Across the entire campus, groups of students could be observed playing all kinds of sports. If you were part of an organized school sport, such as baseball, basketball, track and field, or football, then that practice session usually lasted until around 5:30 when it was again time to return to the main cafeteria. The routine of bells and their ringing at set times orchestrated that evening activity within the dorm, the same as it had for the previous two meals of the day.

Once supper was finished and everyone was back to their individual building, it was time for study hall. That session started with the ringing of another bell. Usually, all the students in a particular dorm gathered in their large assembly hall with numerous chairs and large wooden tables for about an hour and a half. Afterwards, a bell was rung that gave notice it was time for everyone to take a shower. In our dorm, there was one large, tiled area with twelve shower heads. Everyone crowded in, and the space was soon filled with hazy steam and noisy boys for about twenty minutes.

Soon, another bell was rung, indicating it was time to go to bed. Usually that occurred at ten o'clock. All the lights were to be out and everyone quiet within ten minutes.

As you can gather from what I've said, the bells seemed to be never ending. They controlled our lives. In a sense, I believe we all became somewhat institutionalized because of them. The bells took away some of our need to plan and think individually for ourselves about how we should be spending our day.

From my explanation, you can understand why I named this story, "Would someone please stop ringing that bell?" That noise was a daily irritation, but in a small way it became part of our lives.

When I graduated and moved away to college, for the first time in eight years I finally didn't have to live by a bell. In a sense, it was sort of a 'coming of age' time for me, but different. I'd finally grown out of the need to have my life controlled from moment to moment. Whenever I hear a bell ring these days, it brings back memories from my youth. Some of those are good and some of those I'm not so sure how to process. I'm just thankful that part of my life is over.

Mary's Old Homeplace

The human mind is complex and capable of holding secrets for extended periods of time. Those may include old memories, especially dark ones, which can easily surface when least expected and carry us back to a place we'd rather not go. It can happen as quickly as the blinking of an eye.

For Mary, it had been twenty-four years since she'd last seen her old homeplace. Sitting in her vehicle, she stared directly forward completely lost in her thoughts. The vacant structure, nearly one hundred yards farther down a weed-covered dirt driveway, only slightly resembled what it had looked like the last time she set foot on the property. Its unpainted wood siding was beginning to show visible rot near the border of the exposed stone foundation. What had once been a coating of navy-blue paint covering the front door had almost turned an unusual hue of gray from the sun's relentless and blistering heat. Large rust-colored sheets of metal haphazardly clung to the roof, and along the right corner a few of them were curled at the edges from what must have been the result of a strong windstorm. The original glass windowpanes across the front were all broken, leaving a few ragged cloth drapes blowing loosely in the breeze through those openings.

Why she'd come back was still a mystery. Maybe she was struggling to gain a little perspective about her life and what she'd been through, trying to understand it all. It was something she badly needed to do. Within those walls, the old building had at one time served as a refuge throughout early childhood, the only place she really felt safe from the world and its uncertainty. That had all ended suddenly one night, beginning when

Mary was only ten. That's when the sexual abuse from her father began. On that evening, he raped her for the first time of many others that followed. Her mother was only able to semi-protect Mary while being fully aware of the crime that was taking place within their own home. As a result, they both feared for their lives and prayed for a way out of the misery.

At the time, Mary's dad was thirty years old, and her mother was twenty-eight. They'd married eleven years earlier while too young to really have much going in their favor. From the start, it had been a rough road financially, beginning with Mary's birth in the first year.

Her dad could have been a good-looking man of average height and weight, but he didn't take care of himself. He seldom trimmed his unkept, bushy beard and took little pride in his overall appearance, including the clothes he wore. On the other hand, Mary's mom was just the reverse in how she handled herself. She wore clean, ironed dresses and a reasonable amount of makeup around the house. She went to great personal lengths to keep her hair trimmed and combed in a fashionable manner. All of that made her an attractive and desirable woman by any standards.

As Mary slowly stepped out of her car and stared in silence at the decaying place, only confusion and hurt were present in her mind. She could not rid her memory of what her dad had done to her repeatedly while she was only a child.

It had all started with his excessive drinking. Her dad's alcohol problem seemed to manifest itself each night shortly after he arrived home from work at the factory. To hear him talk, it was an unbearable and completely boring job that he hated. He'd open a bottle of Jack Daniel's whiskey and begin to drink soon after entering and closing the front door. It wouldn't be long before he was slurring words and acting erratically as he consumed one straight drink after another. Once that started, his actions were always unpredictable. Usually, they included raw anger that was focused on Mary's mother, which included verbal attacks. Sometimes he'd become physical and slap her multiple times without any obvious remorse. Mary completely feared him and usually went directly to her bedroom on the second floor shortly after he arrived each evening. If possible, she'd usually make up an excuse, so coming down to eat supper was avoided.

Her mother understood and would normally take a plate of food to her to be eaten in the privacy of her bedroom. Once together, they'd whisper quietly and hope he'd fall asleep on the couch in the living room before causing harm to either of them. That didn't happen often enough.

It all came to a head one Friday night when her dad stormed into the bedroom and announced he was planning to kill himself. He stood just inside the doorway holding a double-barreled shotgun and started crying, as both of them watched in complete shock. It was obvious he was very drunk and out of control. Both Mary and her mom begged him to put the gun down and not do anything foolish. He refused and persisted by sitting in a chair, bracing the butt of the gun on the floor between his feet and knees, while pointing the barrel at his chest.

Before anything more could be done, he reached down with his index finger and pulled the trigger. The gun went off, creating a loud, deafening noise, which shook the room. Blood splattered the wall behind him, just before his body fell to the floor.

That fatal event took place so fast, nothing could have stopped him. One moment he was sitting there looking into space with tears running down his face and the next he was lying in a dark red pool of his own blood, staring blankly at the ceiling with open eyes that didn't move. It was more than horrible to have endured.

The police were immediately called, and an ambulance arrived about the same time two officers rushed through the door. What followed was such an emotional time that neither woman was able to fully answer questions without gasping for breath.

The man, Mary's dad, was dead and none of what had happened made any sense to her.

For a long period afterward, time seemed to move forward in a constant mental blur. Mary became increasingly withdrawn with each of those passing years, always feeling as if she lived in a surreal world that could not possibly be authentic. She finally made an effort to consult a psychiatrist shortly after graduating from high school and leaving home, but the expensive meetings didn't seem to help. She was advised that the passage of time would be one of the best ways to heal, but she'd already given that a sufficient effort with no long-term results.

Her mom continued to live in the same house, by herself, and didn't fare much better. She became addicted to prescription drugs given to her for extreme depression. For a while they seemed to help, but with no friends and living in isolation, she spiraled downward and finally hit rock bottom. She died before the age of fifty from an overdose.

As Mary thought back about everything that had happened, she wondered if she'd ever be able to completely let go of the past. What she did know was that the craziness was now over, and she had the chance to be free. Just by having stopped briefly at the home where she'd grown up and having allowed herself to once again mentally sort through those tragic younger years, she'd gained something meaningful that had been missing. It was a better understanding with a new sense of calm. That's what she'd been trying to achieve for many years.

Driving away, there was only one thought which steadfastly remained in her mind, *she was going to make it. Of that, she was entirely sure.*

It was all that really mattered.

The Secret

"Can you keep a secret?" That's what my younger brother asked me early one Saturday morning.

At sixteen and fourteen years of age, we'd always been very close. Whatever one of us was doing, the other one was usually right in the middle of it. We lived in a house that was at least a hundred and fifty years old. It was located not far from town and had a large, fenced yard full of trees in the front but open and flat in the back. Our parents both worked. During the week, Mom was a secretary at a local business in town, and Dad worked at a factory not far away.

I didn't know how to respond to my brother's question at first, other than to ask in return, "Sure...what's going on?"

"I was in the far corner of our garden digging with a shovel yesterday evening trying to plant two small tomato plants and dug up an old leather bag with a drawstring. When I opened it, there were some coins inside. The bag must have been there for a long time because it was nearly rotted through in a few places. In total there's ten gold coins dated from around one hundred years ago. Who do you think might have put them there?"

"I haven't got a clue. It sounds as if they could be quite valuable. Anything in gold these days is worth a lot of money."

"Do you think I should tell Mom or Dad what I've found?"

"Gee...I don't know. If you do that, they'll probably turn the coins in to the police, thinking that's the best way to handle it. Let's take a look at what you have and afterwards I'll let you know my feelings. Why did you decide to tell me about them?"

"Brother…I trust you. I know you wouldn't do me wrong. By the way, if I let you have half of 'em, we'd both be in this together. How'd ya think we can find their real value?"

"Maybe the best thing would be to go to the library downtown and see if there are any books containing photos of old coins that look similar. If we can first identify exactly what they are, we can decide our next move."

"I've got the leather bag in my dresser hidden under a pile of old socks. Let's go take a look. Mom and Dad just left to go to the grocery store, so it'll be a good time."

"Okay, let's go."

"Here they are." He opened the drawstring and lay all ten of them on the bed. "They're each 'bout the size of a fifty-cent piece and quite heavy. They're all the same coins but with different dates from long ago."

"Wow, dude. What you've got here must be worth a fortune. They certainly look like they're made from gold. Nothing shines quite like a coin made from that stuff."

"Why don't we walk downtown to the library and then go to that small coin store located on the corner of Smith and Logan. I've never had a reason to go inside, but I bet the owner can give us an estimated value. He might even exchange the coins for paper money which we can spend."

"Sounds like a plan, brother. We can ride our bikes and get there quicker than walking. Be sure to put that old bag inside a sturdy paper bag so nothing falls out along the way. We don't want to lose any of the coins."

Within ten minutes, we were on our bikes and pedaling toward downtown. Along the way, we decided to skip the library and go directly to the coin store. We were anxious to get the news about the gold and never gave any thought to whether the owner of the store would be willing to keep a secret.

Once inside, there was a middle-aged man behind the counter who looked up and smiled. No one else was in the store.

"What can I do for you two fellows? What brings you to my shop on a Saturday morning?"

"Well, sir," my younger brother said, "I was digging in our yard yesterday and found a leather bag filled with coins. Would you please take a look and see what you think?"

"Sure. That's not a normal request, but it sounds as if you've found something of value. Hand me the bag."

"Here. Inside there are ten of the shiniest coins I've ever seen. They look quite old, but maybe you can tell us what you think."

"Guys, there's no question about it. You've hit the jackpot. These are authentic American gold coins, and the dates prove they're almost one hundred years old. You say you found them buried in your yard. Is that right?"

"Yes, sir. They weren't but about a foot under the surface. Who do you think might have put them there?"

"Don't know, but it must have been someone who lived at your place a long time ago. Maybe they died before they were able to eventually dig them up. Surely, they didn't just forget they were in the ground. Let me look these up in one of my books. I'm fairly sure they'll each be worth at least $1,000 just based on the current value of the metal itself. By the time you consider your gold has already been minted in the form of coins, and very old coins to boot, they may be worth much more."

"Sir, before you go any further, let me ask a serious question. Can this just remain a secret between the three of us? I don't want our parents to know because they'll probably demand we turn them in to the police. That's the way they are...always trying to be honest about everything. We're interested in converting them to money we can spend."

"I don't know. If it remains a secret, plus I give you valuable information including the help to convert them to cash, how about you let me keep one of the coins for all my effort? What'd ya think about that?"

"That sounds fair. But...you've got to promise complete secrecy."

"No problem, as far as I'm concerned. Then it's a done deal. Let's see. I was close to accurate with my first assessment. What you've got are coins worth around $2,000 each on the retail market. I'll give you $10,000 for nine of them and that'll allow me to keep one for myself. The amount of money I'll be paying you will make it possible for me to quickly sell those remaining nine at a wholesale value. I feel sure I won't have any trouble making that happen. Since you two boys won't have to pay any tax on the money, it'll all be free and clear profit. What'd ya think?"

My younger brother looked over at me with a big smile on his face. I was sure all he could think about was what could be bought with the $10,000.

"Let's count it as done, sir. When do we get the cash?"

"I can actually give it to you now. How do you plan to keep your parents from finding out you've got that much money?"

"Now, that's something we haven't considered yet. All of this has happened so quickly we need to give it some thought. What do you suggest?"

"If I were you, I'd hang on to the money and only spend a little of it at a time. Any large purchases will draw suspicion. Like the person who originally hid the coins in the ground, you'll be in that same position. There was a reason those gold coins were never put in the bank."

"I see where you're coming from. Okay, let's do the deal. You take all ten coins, and we get the $10,000."

"Let me see what I've got in my safe. I believe I have enough tens, twenties and fifties to take care of you. That would include a good assortment of lower denominations where you'll never have to go to the bank and draw any attention to your stash. Just a moment and I'll get it all counted out for you."

"I like the way you think, sir. We'll hold on to your cash and only spend a little here and there. Good idea. Thanks."

"Okay, boys, here's the pile of money we agreed on. I'll put it in a small, cloth sack so you can carry it home. Don't spend it all in one place. You know that statement's intended to be nothing but a joke. As we agreed, I'll keep this transaction a secret, if you'll also keep it a secret. Together, we'll all be 'coming out smelling like a bunch of roses,' as I've heard said in the past."

On the way home, we stopped near a park bench, got off our bicycles, and sat down to discuss in private what we now had in our bag.

"Hey…how about that? We made out like bandits. Don't you agree?" I asked.

"Yep…I never figured we'd walk away with $10,000 in cash. Those coins were probably worth even more but why should we be greedy? Now we've got to decide what we can and can't do with the money."

"To be honest, I don't know how in the world we can buy anything which costs very much without our parents questioning where we got the money. If they find out what happened, we may have to give it all up. You and I both do odd jobs for other people during the week, but the wages we receive aren't excessive. Even by saving that money and adding to it our allowances we receive from Mom and Dad, it wouldn't be reasonable that we could buy anything of great value. Looks as if we're stuck with a bag full of cash for now."

"Why don't we get a couple of glass Mason jars with metal tops. We'll put half of the money inside each jar and bury them in a special place in the back yard where no one will ever think to dig. We can always retrieve 'em whenever we need small amounts to buy something special that's reasonably priced and won't cause a problem. Then we can bury the rest back in the ground."

"Truthfully, that's probably all we can do for the time being. In a few years, both of us will be old enough to move out and we'll be off to college in another town. Then, we can take the remaining money with us and spend it in any manner we want. Heck…I might even buy a used car with my share when that happens."

"That's a good plan. Once the jars are buried, I'll feel a little like a pirate with buried treasure. But that'll be between the two of us."

"I appreciate you including me in this deal. You didn't have to do that. Even though we can't freely spend the money, I feel wealthy. Five thousand is the most I've ever had at one time in my life."

"That's what brothers do for each other. You look after me and I'll look after you."

"Now, let's get home, locate two of those jars in the basement, and get the cash in the ground. Let's be sure to take a little for spending purposes, maybe a hundred dollars each. All we've got to do is find a time when Mom and Dad are out again doing errands to get that accomplished."

"Yep…that's important."

"From now on, little brother, I'll be calling you Blackbeard. It'll be our little secret, one pirate to the other."

Buried Treasure

While talking to a good friend recently who owns a landscaping business, he asked, "Ed, have you got the time for me to tell you about a recent discovery made by my employees who were working on a job?"

"Certainly…I'm interested in hearing about it."

"Two weeks ago, I was with a crew of three men while they were hand-digging a narrow trench with shovels, so we could lay a stretch of new plastic pipe to improve the effectiveness of an existing irrigation system. My men were working along a sandy bank of the Intracoastal Waterway at the lower edge of my client's property.

The owner had a mature, live oak tree in that area uprooted by a hurricane. Strong winds pushed it over and left a large, recessed hole in the ground, where the tree's root ball was once located. Our new trench was aligned so that it would run directly through that open hole, requiring us to dig an extra foot deeper.

In the middle of accomplishing that task, one of my workers struck something with his shovel, which made a metallic sound. His first thought was that it might be a metal water pipe that shouldn't be disturbed, so he called me over to investigate.

"I don't know what this is," he said, pointing downward, "but it's right in our way. Hopefully, we can go around or over it in order to properly install our new irrigation pipe. What do you think?"

"Well…the first thing we've got to do is find out exactly what this is. Go ahead and dig a little deeper to expose the object."

"Yes sir."

As his shovel opened a larger area, we discovered that instead of a metal pipe, what was below was a small, rectangular metal box. It was clear that the container had been in the ground for a long time because of all the rust covering its outside. There was an old-fashioned lock connected to a hasp on the front and two sets of discolored brass hinges on the back. They were what held the box's top in place.

"What do you think?" he asked, with a questioning expression on his face.

"Gosh...I don't know. Let's open it. Heck...it could contain treasure. There may be jewelry, coins, or something else of value inside. It looks to be old enough that I'll bet no one is aware it's here."

"Let's do it," he said. "I'll go get a hammer out of my toolbox in the truck, so we can pound off that rusted lock. There's no telling what's inside of this thing."

In less than five minutes, the mystery box was placed on a large rock, and I used the hammer to knock off the lock. It gave way without much effort.

I slowly lifted the lid and peered inside with great anticipation. All three of my employees stood to my side, so that we were crowded tightly together.

"What is that?" one of them asked.

"I don't know, but it's not jewelry or coins, as I hoped. All I see is a dusty, plastic bag. Maybe the best thing to do is take this box and show it to the owner of the property. He needs to know about its existence. You fellows continue working, and I'll do that. I'll let you know what he says."

I walked to the customer's front door and rang his doorbell after shifting the box to one side, which I'd been holding tightly in both of my hands. Along the way, my mind had been busy trying to figure out what it could be. Whatever it was, it had been buried in a strange place by someone in the distant past.

When the door was answered, the owner invited me to come

inside. The box was placed on his kitchen counter and both of us stared blankly at it.

I explained, "This was just found at the bottom of a deep hole in the sand where one of your trees fell near the waterway. At first, I thought we'd found some long-lost treasure, but it only contains a bag with something odd inside. Do you have an idea what this could be?"

The man looked at me with a perplexed expression on his face, and shrugged his shoulders, indicating he had no clue what it was or what it contained. Then, he began to lean forward and move closer and closer to the box. All at once, there was a slight smile that appeared on his face, which was completely unexpected.

He ran his fingers carefully over the surface of the rusted box, just before saying, "Well...I'll be damned. That's my ex-mother-in-law! She died almost forty years ago. She lived with us shortly after we married and always loved the waterway near the back of our house. We had her cremated and her ashes placed in a bag. That bag was sealed and put inside this metal box, which we buried. Above it, a tree was planted to mark the spot. I'd completely forgotten about it. My wife and I divorced around twenty years ago, and she's currently married to another guy."

"I'm glad you recognized it," I responded. "What do you plan to do with the box now?"

"I guess the best thing to do is give her a phone call. We don't really get along, even after all the years which have passed since we split up. It was a nasty divorce. I'll do that right now."

As I stood to one side of the room, he placed a telephone call to his ex-wife.

I heard him say, "Mary, this is Harold. I had some excavation work done in the backyard today. The landscaper was digging a trench to run additional water lines for my irrigation system. A large tree had fallen, due to the recent storm, leaving a big hole in the ground right where they were digging. They found the metal box in which your mother's ashes were buried. It has to be moved because it's in the way. If you want it, come and get it. If you don't come soon, I'm going to throw it away."

After that was said, I assumed from his reaction that she'd immediately hung up on him. He laid the phone down and just shook his head from side to side, indicating to me that she was a strange individual, for which he didn't have any remaining affectionate feelings. There was nothing more I could do, so I left the house and walked back down to where my workers were busy digging other parts of the trench. I quickly related to them what had happened.

In less than twenty minutes, we heard a siren blaring in the distance and saw a police car pulling up to the front of the house with its blue lights flashing. After turning those off, the policeman left his car and disappeared into the house. He was there for only a short time before getting back in his patrol car and leaving.

It was obvious all of my men were curious to know what had taken place, but they continued to work. Because I was also curious, I walked to the house, knocked on the door, and was let inside.

"What in the world was that all about?" I asked.

"It seems that Mary over-reacted...it's the same type of emotional response she always displayed over simple matters before we finally split. Once I let her know that if she didn't come and get her mother's ashes, I was going to throw them away, she went nuts. Called the cops and told them I was planning to destroy private property...her mother's ashes.

I told the cop that it was a civil matter, between my ex-wife and myself, and not something in which he needed to be involved. He agreed, once he knew the facts. He advised me to return the box to her and not destroy it in order to avoid any further problems. I assured him that was what I planned to do."

He then shook my hand, smiled, and said, "I was married

once myself. You're in an awkward position, which I understand. Sounds like you made a good decision to divorce that woman. Instead of her being sensible when you let her know about the box that had been found after forty years in the ground, she wanted to cause you trouble by calling us. Do yourself a favor by giving her nothing more to complain about," the officer added.

I said to Harold, "I'm sorry we caused you to get in the middle of all this. I didn't know anything else to do but show you the box."

"Don't worry about it. Actually, I sort of enjoyed the whole encounter. It reminded me, once again, that I made the right decision long ago. Since our divorce, my world has been much more peaceful, and I've enjoyed each day to the fullest without her involvement. Let's get that irrigation system fixed, so that issue can be taken off my list of concerns."

"You got it! It would have been more fun if that old box had been filled with jewelry and coins, but not every day can include that much excitement. What you've just experienced is enough. I'm going to get back to work with my crew. By tomorrow evening, we should have your irrigation system functioning properly, so we can move on to deal with someone else's issues. Nice to be of assistance. Call us again, if we can help."

"Will do. Thanks for everything you're getting done for me."

I left the house and walked toward my crew, as the three of them stopped working, turned, and began to stare. They understandably wanted to know what had just occurred. They formed a half circle in front of me, and I relayed the story exactly as it had been told by Harold. Together, we had a good laugh, knowing it really wasn't something in which we should have found quite that much humor...but in spite of that fact, all of us enjoyed the moment.

I said, "Okay, we've had our fun. Let's get back to work. I want this project completed by midday tomorrow. I feel sure there's another crisis waiting to be dealt with as soon as this job is finished."

Satisfied with my explanation and what I'd just said, all three men picked up their shovels and continued to dig the trench.

Know there are obstacles everywhere.
They're more common than most
of us realize.

Therefore, choose your own path through life.
Only by using your God-given common sense
and logic will you be able to overcome
and achieve real success.

Ed Hearn

The Mystery of Genius

Last evening, I watched a program hosted by William Shatner who has recently taken on the role of narrating a few science-oriented presentations for the History Channel. He's the same guy who starred in the Star Trek series years ago, beginning in the 60s. Currently, he's in his nineties and still going strong. The clear and distinctive tone of his voice, plus the timing of his delivery, make what he's now doing very interesting.

As I sat watching and listening to him, he talked about the mystery of genius. That subject instantly got my attention. Early in the program, one of his examples was the genius of the Wright brothers, Orville and Wilbur. He pointed out how immensely their genius has benefited our entire society, and mankind as a whole, over the last century. The fact they progressed beyond operating a simple bicycle repair shop, to building and getting the first crude airplane to fly, is hard to believe. Their incredible innovations allowed them to solve the age-old mystery of powered flight. Much of what we take for granted these days, from commercial airliners to space shuttles, can be traced back to those two ordinary brothers and their unlikely stroke of genius.

Similar genius is also evident with many other inventions that have been created, and accomplishments that have been achieved, by special people with an unbelievably high intellect. That includes the field of mathematics and physics; as was the case with Albert Einstein; music, as with Beethoven and Mozart; and memory, as was the case with a well-known savant named Laurence Kim Peek who died in 2009. He had the ability to perform incredible mental feats that no one else on earth could do. One of those included him being able to quote any specific passage he was asked about from the 12,000 books he'd read during his lifetime. Also, there are well-known inventors, such as Thomas Edison and Steve Jobs who fall into that category, along with famous artists, such as Leonardo DaVinci, and numerous other childhood prodigies.

Shatner posed the question during his presentation, "Could it be true that we're all put on this earth with the capability to do something extraordinary?" He went on to say, "It's an inspiring thought and suggests that each of us has his own brand of genius. That's one of the things scientists are now exploring when it comes to all the varied forms of genius. They suggest that a lot of untouched potential definitely exists in each of our brains. It's a fact that we all have the hidden potential for genius locked deep within our minds. The trick is to find a way to systematically access that ability. It's just a matter of discovering a way to tap into it. If we could do that, there's no telling how many amazing things we could create and how many discoveries we could make for the benefit of the human race."

According to a website on the Internet named 'MyOxbridge,' here's what they say about people who are considered to be genius:

"Being a genius isn't as simple as just being smart or having a high IQ. While intelligence is, of course, a prerequisite of genius status, there are other things at play. Those include creativity, an increased self-awareness, and an innate ability to ask questions few others have ever asked.

It's for that reason that the likes of Einstein, Steven Hawking, and Charles Darwin can be placed in the same genius pool as Mozart, Beethoven, and Picasso. Even though on paper those preeminent figures are worlds apart, they still shared a similar knack for pushing the boundaries of human thought and our understanding of the world.

Defining genius isn't easy, but it's safe to say that intelligence, creativity, and outside-the-box thinking all play their part in making a person considered a genius...a true genius.

Those recognized in that special category are regularly pigeonholed. They do, however, share similar traits and characteristics, each contributing to their ability to see the world differently than all of us regular folks.

Four key characteristics that define a true genius begin with a curious mind. It stands to reason that a person needs to possess a high degree of curiosity to achieve excellence. By having an inquisitive nature, those people are more likely to develop new ways of thinking and uncover previously unexplored ideas. Individuals deemed to be a genius may pursue knowledge in an almost obsessive manner, beyond what the average person may consider reasonable.

The second major characteristic that defines a genius is that they are usually abstract thinkers. They tend to think about problems and concepts in a much more dynamic way. As a result, they are unlikely to accept information and facts on face value. Instead, they will want to defy and test conventional thinking. Talking to someone who possesses genius traits can be tricky, as they may want to challenge your personal way of thinking, which more than likely differs radically from theirs.

The third characteristic is that those people are usually risk-takers. Being truly innovative, they will want to push boundaries. They'll not be satisfied taking the safe route, especially if they feel they are close to making a breakthrough discovery. That approach to life can sometimes mean they put themselves at risk, whether physically or in regard to the progression of their career, but ultimately that course of action can lead to groundbreaking accomplishments.

A fourth characteristic is that they usually reject routine. They may find it hard to conform to a normal routine, possibly because they constantly have ideas and questions running through their minds. Very often those who achieve greatness are also nocturnal and will continue to explore their ideas at all hours and come up with solutions while everyone else is fast asleep."

What I gained by listening carefully to the program, as it was presented last evening, was an answer to Shatner's question. Yes...undoubtedly we're all capable of doing something extraordinary. What we have to individually discover is exactly what that might be for each of us. Since we're normally using only a very small percentage of our brain, there's a lot more potential available. All that's needed is to push ourselves and discover what we're really capable of achieving.

Micro World of the Very Small

While recently wandering through our local Barnes and Noble bookstore in search of something interesting, I noticed a new book published by Smithsonian. The book was oversized and thick, with a large photo on its cover jacket of a tiny ant interacting with a droplet of water. The scene's intricate details were only visible as the result of a camera attached to a specialized macro lens. Because I've always been interested in science and nature, I was quickly drawn to it with a great amount of curiosity.

After retrieving the book off its shelf, my next move was to locate a comfortable chair in order to relax while exploring the contents. I was quickly captivated by actual color photos and complex drawings including all types of tiny creatures, some of which I never knew existed.

I noticed microscopic life-forms shown in extreme close-ups, revealing details such as human nerve cells and hair follicles. There was a section showing overlooked groups that have a huge role in the natural world. That included insects, which make up approximately 80% of the world's animal species, plus bacteria about which was stated, "There's more in a human's mouth than there are people in the entire world." From the tiniest spiders and insects to even microscopic creatures like bacteria and viruses, I was able to see in great detail such things as the beauty of a pollen grain, a butterfly egg, and the spore of a common fungus.

There were close-up images of dust mites, fleas, ticks, lice, gnats, no-see-'ums, and many other inhabitants of a world so small that most of us are unaware they live and surround us daily. Some of them move around by using fragile, jointed legs with claws at the end and others propel themselves in water with the help of tiny hairs surrounding their bodies. There were a few shown that contained strange heads with compound eyes and odd shaped mouths. No matter how weird, they all possess a specialized way to eat for nourishment. Some of the creatures are able to take in nutrients by attaching themselves to other living things with the aid of feeder tubes or highly complex suction devices.

Of each species, there were both male and females shown with different body parts. Sometimes their individual body coloring varied from one sex to the other. With each page turned, I became more fascinated with what the book contained and what was offered to see and learn.

One complete section discussed and displayed photos of complex viruses, fungi, molds, and microscopic living things which can do us harm. Most of those react in a similar way in order to survive. Viruses are able to attach themselves to their host using a variety of techniques. Some contain harpoon-type projections for that purpose, similar to short hairs with a sharp point, that stick into a living creature's flesh. That can either take place within a host's body or on an outside area and holds them in place while they inject harmful compounds and enzymes. Other types of viruses attach by using a sucker-type method before becoming a problem. Fungi and molds have evolved with their own methods of attaching to various living matter for the purpose of removing sustenance, so they can survive and reproduce.

A part of the book dealt with extremely small creatures such as one-celled animals. That included amoebas and paramecium. I found those very interesting because the photos took me back to many years ago when I was in high school biology class. One day we were allowed to use a microscope to view a fresh drop of pond water. It was a random sample but completely saturated with so much life I was astounded. There were numerous amoebas which were basically clear in color and obviously aggressive. As small, transparent blobs, they moved slowly through the water hunting for something to devour. Whenever another living creature was touched, it was soon surrounded and absorbed. The paramecium reacted similarly; in that they were also hunters. Their one-celled bodies moved by the rhythmic rotation of what appeared to be tiny hairs surrounding an outer surface.

I was also reminded of a time nearly thirty years ago when I owned a Nikon camera with an extreme close-up, macro lens attachment. I'd purchased that special and expensive piece of photographic equipment, along with a heavy-duty tripod, to be able to view and photograph very small things. Once it was set up, I began to look around for items so tiny they were normally ignored by most people. That included objects such as a flower petal saturated with pollen dust, a dead ant with bizarre body parts, bits of small leaves containing intricate canals where fluids could circulate, the transparent wing of a house fly, grains of sand, and other similar substances.

Those were placed, one at a time, beneath the lens of my camera where I could adjust the focus and depth of field to view a particular part. Beyond just having the ability to see it, as if I were observing through an expensive laboratory microscope, I could also snap a color photo so later it could be enlarged.

Some of those unusual enlargements were found to be of interest to the editor of a local magazine. Before I knew it, a few of my choice shots had been published to go along with articles he'd written, which in various ways tied back to the photos. I was always given written credit for my images when used with his articles. It was an ego trip I enjoyed for the better part of a year, before I finally tired of providing him with the photography in return for a meager amount of money.

What I've just talked about is the reason I found the book at Barnes and Noble so engaging. It took me back to the past and reminded me of a world I'd almost forgotten. If you think you might be interested, stop by that store and take a look for yourself. The book is titled, *Micro Life: Miracles of the Miniature World Revealed,* with a bold, dark purple cover jacket, and sells for slightly less than fifty dollars.

Marching to the Beat of Your Own Drum

Throughout my life, I've heard a friendly comment made about me having to do with how others view the way I live, which has stood out to me as memorable. So intriguing, and in its own way uniquely complimentary was the comment, that somewhere along the way I started believing it must be true. At first, it took me a while to accept that the comment actually fit my personality, due to the fact it could be taken as either positive or negative. Later on, I began viewing what was said in only a positive manner, connected with a little personal pride.

In saying that, I realize my ego is talking. Maybe a few of those people really meant what they said in a negative light. I hope not. Everyone sees things differently. No two people are the same. We're all unique and our personalities have been formed throughout our lives due to everything we've had to go through and experience, so we could finally arrive in the current moment.

Enough said about that. Here's the exact comment I'm referring to: "You seem to be a person who marches to the beat of your own drum." That simple but blunt statement has never offended me in the least.

In thinking about it, I decided to look up what was said on the Internet. Following is the actual passage from *Walden,* as written by Henry David Thoreau, which is usually considered the origin of that particular expression: "Why should we be in such desperate haste to succeed, and in such desperate enterprises? If a man does not keep pace with his companions, perhaps it is because he hears a different drummer. Let him step to the music which he hears, however measured or far away. It is not important that he should mature as an apple tree or an oak."

Also, taken directly from Thoreau's work of *Walden,* written in 1854, is a poem he wrote about the same subject:

"Marching to the beat of your own drum,
A rhythm unique, a path unchartered.
In a world of conformity, you stand apart,
With courage and conviction, you follow your heart.

The cadence of your steps, a melody so free,
Guided by intuition, where no one else can see.
You dance to your tune, a symphony of one,
Embracing the journey, under the same old sun.

Through valleys and peaks, you forge your way,
Leaving footprints of resilience, day by day.
The beat of your drum echoes across time,
A legacy woven in rhythm, sublime.

So keep marching, my friend, with unwavering grace,
For your unique rhythm is a gift to this space.
And as you tread boldly, remember the truth soon:
The world needs more drummers who dance to their own tune."

With continued research on the Internet about the same subject, here's additional information of interest I found in the form of an explanation:

"The idiom, 'March to the beat of one's own drum,' or the very similar, 'March to the beat of a different drummer,' means someone who is unconventional, a nonconformist, or a person who does things in his or her own way. Whether that is a positive or negative characteristic depends on what exactly is being referred to, and perhaps even more on the attitude of the person making the comment.

Some people value conformity highly and tend to see those

who violate norms as selfish or antisocial. Other people think of the ability to make one's own choice to indicate bravery or praiseworthy resistance to the pressure of the majority."

All of my research, as noted above, was both interesting and meaningful. I found that in conclusion, I'm a little different in the way I choose to handle my life, but I'm not alone. I know there's some real sanity connected with being my own person and living my life on my own terms. As long as I can keep from offending others, and they understand my quirks, no one else should really care.

Make Good Things Happen

Have you ever considered how important it really is to make the most of each day and every moment in your life?

This morning, while taking a quiet walk around the neighborhood, I began to think about those two things. They are both important to keep in mind as we rush through our lives of work, family, and responsibilities. We're always trying to get the most out of life while dealing with the pressures and stresses that can't be avoided.

Sometimes, we need to just stop and think in depth about what we're doing with our available time. We should be the ones in control of how we use each moment and should fill our days with activities of real importance, even though the world occasionally appears to be making those decisions for us and controlling the outcome.

I find myself frequently thinking about how to accomplish the most with each new day. Often, I fall short with my efforts and end up trying to decide why I wasted so much of my valuable time pursuing the wrong course of action. On the other hand, when something worthwhile is accomplished, it's nice to be able to end the day with an inner pride about how the hours were used to either my advantage or to the benefit of others.

I realize that each day should start with a clean slate. But in fact, we're all somewhat influenced, or even possibly constrained, by how we left the past day or past weeks. In spite of that truth, we can still make good things happen. That's human nature at its best. We should never focus backward on negative things but be constantly reaching forward to make something special out of the future.

There's a lesson in all these thoughts that borders on simplicity. It centers on the idea of 'carpe diem,' which means 'to seize the day.' That's become my personal goal when beginning each morning, and I intend to continue along that path throughout my remaining lifetime.

Good Books with Good Endings

If you're like me, you enjoy searching for and eventually finding a good book that can be read in your spare time, that offers unique content in the form of stories, or memories, to which you can relate. Sometimes your intention is just to find a novel to read for pleasure with the goal of short-term mental escape, but your search can also lead to a world that's completely unexpected.

On occasion, I visit our local Barnes and Noble bookstore to spend a few productive hours surfing though racks and racks filled with recently published or old titles that grab my attention. There seems to be no end to what's available. Without fail, during each trip, there will be at least three or four books that demand I take a closer look. To avoid having to buy any of those without first checking them out thoroughly, I normally sit in a chair toward the front of the store and speed-read volume after volume. Anything of great interest is then purchased so it can be reread in greater detail at home.

I've enjoyed for years the opportunity to read a growing list of interesting novels written by diversified and talented authors, including stories of fiction and non-fiction. When one of their well-told narratives nears the last few paragraphs of the final chapter, I love it if the creator has skillfully inserted a few of his own deep, inner thoughts as a conclusion. Those thoughts are usually intended to linger in the reader's mind and sum up what he's been trying to get across within the main story. Some of those endings I remember well into the future, and often they cause me to go back to the beginning to reread portions of the book because of his final mind-provoking comments.

For me, that's the signature indicator a novel has real, lasting substance. Below I'll give you two of those endings as examples of what I'm saying. Each of which I've held in my memory for a long time, and they both have a special meaning to me.

In Nelson DeMille's popular novel from 2002, titled *Up Country,* he ended with this statement:

"The journey home is never a direct route; it is, in fact, always circuitous, and somewhere along the way, we discover that the journey is more significant than the destination, and that people we meet along the way will be traveling companions of our memories forever."

I like not only what DeMille said in that concluding paragraph in his book, but I admire the way in which he worded it. Whenever an author can successfully remind his reader of a particular fact as a well-written conclusion, which is personal for both individuals, he's then touched that individual's heart in an unusual way that will never be forgotten. I do agree with his statement above and think that we all eventually discover life's journey is far more significant than its ultimate destination, and that the people we meet along the way are destined to always remain in our memories.

In Norman MaClean's book written in 1976, which later became a Hollywood movie, titled *A River Runs Through It,* the closing statement is:

"It is those we live with and love and should know, who elude us. Now…nearly everyone I loved and did not understand when I was young are dead, but I still reach out to them. Of course, now I am too old to be much of a fisherman and usually fish the big waters alone, although some friends think I shouldn't. Like many fly fishermen in western Montana where the summer days are almost Arctic in length, I often do not start fishing until the cool of the evening. In the Arctic half-light of the canyon, all existence fades to a single being within my soul. There are specific memories and sounds of the Big Blackfoot River, intensified by the four-count rhythm, as I work my flyrod with the hope a fish will rise…Eventually, all things merge into one, and a river runs through it. The river was cut by the world's great flood and runs over rocks from the basement of time. On some of those rocks are timeless raindrops. Under the rocks are the words, and some of the words are theirs. I am haunted by waters."

Above are the thoughts of an old man who fished one specific river with his brother and father, as a youth, and later throughout his entire life. He's reflecting on all he's been through after both of the others have died and left him alone. His thoughts, as he stands by himself with a flyrod in his hand, slowly casting into the clear water and waiting for a trout to rise and take his lure, are centered around what he's learned about himself and his existence from that river, his father, and his brother. It's a touching scene, not only in the book, but in the movie as well.

In my personal life, I have a similar connection to fishing with family members who have now died. Memories of their past existence relate to the waters of a special lake in middle Tennessee which ran through the center of our lives and seemed to hold our family together for many years.

I am also 'haunted by those waters.'

*If you're lucky enough
to retire in good health,
search out new hobbies and interesting people
with which you can spend your time.*

*Being involved in a variety of activities
with special friends is a gift available to older individuals.
Take advantage of the opportunity.*

*Remember: A good friend is invaluable
and not to be taken lightly.*

Ed Hearn

A Bluebird Story – Box #9

Bluebird nesting season was fast approaching on a cold day in March of 2021. George Wesoloski was aware of the tedious work his wife Judy normally completed during the season, while updating a data monitoring book for twenty of the bluebird boxes on the Marsh golf course in Landfall. After compiling her annual collection of information each year, Judy would report the gathered statistics to the North Carolina Bluebird Society.

Her monitoring book consisted of twenty numbered pages, one for each bluebird box that had been assigned to her care. All the weekly information was recorded there, and it included the date a new nest had been built, its current condition, the number of eggs, the number of babies born alive, feather cover, etc.

George found the previous year's book among Judy's things at their house. Inside, he added twenty new numbered pages and prepared a monitoring bag with the necessary tools: a trowel, a long-handled brush, an empty plastic bag for cleaning out old nesting material, as well as a pen and a pencil with an eraser.

On that day, two couples had decided to assist him with the task, Walter and Angela Skinner along with John and Pam McNeill. While traveling in golf carts from box to box around the golf course, George informed them of Judy's current condition, and that he was temporarily taking over her responsibilities.

Halfway through his spring chore of inserting clean fiber cups in the bluebird boxes on the golf course, he opened box number nine. Inside, there was a dead adult bluebird. The sight shocked him. It was not normal to find a previously healthy adult in that condition. All the boxes had been emptied and cleaned in the fall of the previous year.

At the time, George's wife, Judy, was in her second week of intensive care at New Hanover Regional Hospital fighting for her life. A cerebral hemorrhage had left her paralyzed on her right side. She was heavily sedated. A ventilator had been keeping her alive and made it impossible for her to speak. Holding her hand at the bedside later that day, George pondered...was the dead bluebird he'd just discovered an omen of what might be coming?

For the next week, George, his son, and two daughters kept a vigil at Judy's bedside. The stroke she'd suffered turned out not to be survivable. The dead bluebird in box number nine had, in fact, told of her fate. She passed away only a few days after it had been found.

Her long-term dedication to the propagation of bluebirds will be remembered. When you see a bluebird in your yard in Landfall, think about Judy Wesoloski.

Landfall's Memorial Garden

Next to the Kenan Chapel in Landfall is the Memorial Garden, where residents may place their loved one's ashes to honor their memories.

George Wesoloski decided to do something significant to honor the memory of his wife Judy, because of the commitment she'd had to the long-term bluebird project within the community. He solicited help from Ed Hearn, a local bronze sculptor, who was a fellow resident and neighbor. Together, they came up with an idea for a lasting memorial to be placed within those gardens. It would be Hearn's third major, bronze sculpture to be placed there on permanent outdoor display. After submitting final drawings for the project to a committee at the Chapel, George and Ed were given the go-ahead to proceed.

The approved plan was to create a realistic bluebird nest box held up by a weathered post with two life-size birds, all in bronze. One bird would be in the process of emerging from the nesting hole in the box, while another would be standing on the top left edge. There would be a large, natural boulder placed to the right side of the bluebird box with a third bluebird perched on its top corner looking across and up at the other two birds, along with a bronze plaque. That plaque was to read, "To the memory of 'The Bluebird's Best Friend'- Judy Wesoloski."

To add to the overall sculpture's visual effect, three additional bronze bluebirds would be placed on the top edges of existing, smaller boulders in the general area. Those were intended to be subtle but enough to carry the theme of the memorial outward.

This memorial was designed to be a continuing reminder of Judy's fascination and dedication to the propagation of bluebirds in the Landfall neighborhood. There is also a regular wood blue-bird box, with the number eighteen on its side, located near the lady's ninth tee on the Marsh course with a small brass plaque containing her name.

The main bronze sculpture was officially dedicated at the Memorial Garden on Saturday, April 16, 2022.

The Bluebird of North Carolina

The unusually beautiful eastern bluebird has been in decline in North Carolina. Human activities, pesticides, the reduction of grasslands, and the introduction of aggressive species have all contributed to reducing the cavity nesting sites for this popular bird. An effort is currently underway by the North Carolina Bluebird Society (*ncbluebird.org*) to increase the bluebird population by educating the public on how to be a 'Bluebird Landlord."

Numerous organizations and clubs in this state have started projects to attract these birds to their area. It may be to their local parks, golf courses, or their backyards. Getting started is not hard but requires following a few special procedures and just a little knowledge about the birds. First, bluebirds prefer an open area such as a grassland, with a few interspersed trees. Second, they prefer a properly sized nest box with a 1 ½ inch opening, placed approximately five feet off the ground on a circular pole or square post. You should never place one of these nesting boxes on the side of a tree, as predators such as snakes and squirrels can too easily access the box. A baffle halfway up the pole is an easy way to ward off most of them. Third, you will need to monitor the box every week during the nesting season, March through August, because the birds will nest more than one time during a season.

In February and March, bluebirds begin to actively search for a suitable place to build a nest. The nest is usually made of pine straw and will be built within some type of cavity where the babies gain protection. In early to mid-March, the original nest will appear. Once the mother lays her first egg, she will continue to lay an additional blue egg every day until there are either four or five.

She may not immediately sit on the eggs, but eventually she'll start to incubate them with her body heat. Approximately fourteen days later, the eggs will hatch within hours of each other. The adults, male and female, will begin to feed the babies. Hatchlings grow very fast and are enjoyable to observe. If viewing, be sure to carefully open the box door for only a brief amount of time. The babies will usually leave the nest in about eighteen days, within just a few hours of each other.

Monitoring is fun, if you're interested. The North Carolina Bluebird Society provides a standard monitoring sheet to easily follow the weekly progression. Bluebirds don't mind having their box opened occasionally for the weekly inspection. Just be careful while opening it, as one of the adults may suddenly fly out. Once the young have fledged and left the nest, it should be cleaned. If this is done, the adults will soon return to the empty box to begin their cycle once again. Two nestings in a season are typical. Occasionally, a third nesting may happen before the season ends near the end of August or early September.

Hobnobbing with the Rich and Famous

In March of 2024, I upgraded to a newer car. A brand-new one was not purchased, because I honestly don't believe making a financial move like that would be smart on my part. As most people know, as soon as a new car is driven away from the dealership, it depreciates at least ten thousand dollars, if not more. For that reason, the car I chose was a 2020 model.

To now own a five-year newer vehicle than I had before, a completely unblemished Lexus SUV with brand new tires and an extended factory warranty, was good enough for me. It only had 19,800 miles on its odometer. We've all heard the saying, which explains in a humorous way, why a particular car of obvious age has remained in very good condition with low miles. It goes like this: 'That vehicle was previously owned by a little old lady who only drove it to the mailbox to pick up her mail and then back to her garage, without ever leaving her own driveway.' With the car I recently bought, that situation could have easily been the case, because it was so free of any issues that the automobile could have been purchased right off the showroom floor from the same dealership, where I located it in their used car lot.

While removing all personal items from my older SUV trade-in, including all the stuff that had accumulated in its glove compartment over six and a half years, I found a stack of old CDs which I hadn't listened to in probably five years. One of them on top of that pile caught my eye. It was the first official CD recording put out by Sara Evans. She'd hit the Nashville country music market in a whirlwind many years earlier and became an instant celebrity.

For old times sake, I inserted the CD into my car's player and listened again. Its first song was one I remembered well and instantly brought back memories with meaningful lyrics. The name was, *These are the Moments*. As I listened, I couldn't help but sing along.

Following are three of the lines taken from that recording: *These are the moments... I thank God that I'm alive. These are the moments...I'll remember all my life. I've found all that I've waited for, and I could not ask for more.* With musical instruments adding a harmonious melody, along with Sara's beautiful voice, I sat transfixed while running her words through my mind. In fact, they tugged at my heart, as they have done with many other individual's emotions who've listened to that song since the tune was first released. Her words were powerful. I agree with what was said and believe that 'these are the moments,' and we should be 'remembering them for the rest of our lives.' We should be living in the present. She was also correct in the fact that if we honestly thank God for what we enjoy in each and every moment, there should be little else necessary to request from Him.

I've given you that background and would now like to include a short bit of additional information you might find interesting. Sara Evans moved to Nashville, Tennessee around twenty years ago with hopes of becoming part of the country music business. When she first arrived in that city, no one knew who she was. While she waited for her big break and gradually met key individuals who listened to her recorded demo tapes and began to promote her, she needed a regular job and found one working for my younger brother. She was his main receptionist in the front office, greeting visitors and answering the phone. Her destiny was soon to change. Before long, a few of her recordings were professionally converted into copies of the CD I was listening to. Song after song was played on national radio stations, with instant popularity throughout the United States. As you probably know, she's now a huge contemporary country music star, highly respected, and making big money.

I found it interesting that my brother was able to personally help her financially before she got fully established in the music industry.

Another story relayed to me by my brother involved a different country music personality you'll remember.

One late evening, after dark, he was driving home while using the busy Interstate. To the side of the road, he noticed in his headlights a new Cadillac pulled off on the shoulder with an older man standing beside it. He knew there had to be an obvious problem taking place. He decided to stop and see if there was a way he could be of assistance.

After parking at least ten feet off the road, my brother walked over to meet the individual to see what he could do. The man welcomed him with great relief by saying, "I recently purchased this car, and it now has a flat tire. Will you please help me?"

Seeing a man of advanced age without a flashlight, it was obvious the fellow was in no condition to safely change the tire. His wife was accompanying him but had remained inside the Cadillac.

Following a brief discussion, the decision was made for my brother to drive both of them to their home, which they said was located only a few miles away. The man said, "I'll deal with this problem tomorrow by calling a wrecker to take the car back to the dealership for the necessary repair. It's too dangerous to try and change a tire on the edge of the Interstate."

Just before letting them out at their home, the man finally introduced himself, by saying, "I'm Eddie Arnold. You probably know of me because of some of my music."

"Yes...I'm well aware of who you are," my brother replied. "You're the famous country music legend. I'm so glad to meet you. Above all, I'm glad to be able to help."

Eddie Arnold repeatedly thanked my brother for his generosity and offered to pay him for his assistance. The money was refused. Just knowing he'd been of help to a man who was an icon within the country music industry was enough to satisfy my brother.

During the many years I lived in the Nashville area, I also experienced a few personal encounters with some of the various country music entertainers. Here's my story about one of those:

Occasionally, after spending all day at my business, I'd stop at a popular buffet restaurant located approximately halfway to my home for some good ole country cooking. On one memorable evening, there was an older man standing in line just in front of me with a much younger lady at his side. Being an extrovert who loves to strike up a conversation with just about anyone, I engaged them in conversation with a friendly comment. It was taken well, and before we even made it to the beginning of the serving line, I felt that both individuals were interested in talking in more detail. As a result, they asked me to join them at their table, so we could continue what we were discussing.

Without hesitation, I took them up on the offer. It wasn't long after we were seated and enjoying ourselves that the man introduced himself. He said, "I'm Roy Acuff. I live alone in a nice home provided by, and located on, the Opryland property, and my granddaughter here occasionally picks me up and brings me to this restaurant for a healthy dinner."

Stunned, I replied, "I'm Ed Hearn. Am I correct that you're Roy Acuff, the famous entertainer who sang the song, *Wabash Cannonball,* for years on end, as part of the regular Grand Ole Opry's weekly production, along with numerous other famous hits?"

"That's me," he said. "I'm now in my nineties and those days are mostly behind me. I've had an interesting life."

What followed was a spirited conversation with a grateful man who obviously loved life. I'll never forget that evening. In the following months, I ate dinner with the two of them several times, and on each occasion our running into each other occurred strickly by chance. Whenever he saw me in line, he'd invite me to come over to his table.

Another, and completely separate encounter with a popular entertainer, occurred during the final day of my divorce after thirty years of marriage. It took place in a small town located thirty miles outside of Nashville by the name of Gallatin, which was close to where I lived in Hendersonville, Tennessee.

Having arrived early at the courthouse and standing with my attorney, he asked, "I know this is a sad day for you, but would you be interested in going into the courtroom to sit through the divorce of a famous Nashville country music entertainer? That proceeding will be occurring just before yours on the docket."

With nothing else to do, he'd piqued my interest. What followed was the official ending of Trisha Yearwood's marriage to her former husband, so she could later marry Garth Brooks. I sat through the whole proceeding and watched in amazement. Once it was over, my case came before the judge. While it was taking place, I thought once or twice about Trisha and figured she'd probably not hung around to sit in on my divorce, as I'd done with hers.

One more interesting personality that I'll mention involved a famous entertainer who lived no more than one-eighth of a mile from where my parents owned a small home on the edge of Old Hickory Lake in Hendersonville. There was a boat dock in our backyard where our small boat was moored. While still in my teens and during an early Saturday morning, I used that small boat and paddled to the far side of a nearby cove to fish the nearby banks for largemouth bass. Getting out on the water, shortly after the sun had started to rise above the horizon, was the best time. As I worked my way with the paddle along a rock cliff face that dropped off quickly to deep water, I repeatedly cast my lure within a foot of the edge and let it sink while lightly jerking the tip of my rod to entice a big bass.

Out of the corner of my eye, there was movement on a nearby dock and a man dressed in solid black asked in a friendly voice, "Are you catching anything, son?"

"Nope," I replied, "but I'm having fun. Beautiful morning, don't you agree?"

"That it is. I'm down here at my dock early this morning, so I can take my motorboat out for a quiet ride. I'm usually out of town entertaining. This is a rare occasion, so I'm planning to take advantage of the opportunity."

"Aren't you Johnny Cash?" I asked.

"That's correct. I have this nice home that was built on the edge of this cliff but seldom get to fully enjoy it. June, my wife, and I stay on the road most of the time. Where do you live?"

"We live just around the corner. I've known you lived here for some time but have never seen either you or your wife. Doesn't Roy Orbison live next to you in that big house?"

"That's again correct. He also travels a lot. Because of that, we don't see each other very often. He's famous. You know that don't you?"

"I'm well aware that both of you guys are famous. It's great seeing you this morning. I'll be sure to tell my friends that I met Johnny Cash."

"Well…whatever you do, remember that I'm just like everyone else. Some of us gain a favored degree of notoriety for one reason or the other, while others go basically unnoticed in this life. We're all part of God's children. You take care. I'm glad we met this morning."

With that said, I paddled on down the bank and continued to fish. Johnny boarded his motorboat, started its engine, and quickly disappeared after moving across the main channel and leaving behind only a wake which slowly rocked my boat.

Following that day, Johnny became more and more popular but also suffered from drug addiction and depression. I guess that was all part of him becoming so famous and his attempt to understand his life. Those feelings were reflected in later songs which he wrote and recorded.

I still hear some of his songs played on the radio, television, and used in a few movies. Each time that happens, memories of our unexpected encounter on that unusual morning come to mind.

When in doubt,
examine deep inside and question
your inner self.

You have a subconscious morality which
was established over many years
and should be trusted as a reliable
source for future direction.

Ed Hearn

Lost in Transition

Have you ever found yourself in the situation where something really important disappeared, and you had no idea what happened to it?

This morning, I passed by a friend named Paul, while walking my dog. We quickly got into a short conversation about his recent trip to New York, where he'd traveled to help his son move from one location to the other.

As Paul related his story, he began by telling me, "There was a point during that trip when I couldn't find my car keys. My first thought was that I must have locked them inside my car the last time I'd taken a load of his things and placed them inside. Panic swept over me while considering my dilemma. As I frantically searched through everything outside the vehicle, my keys thankfully fell to the ground from an empty satchel bag that I picked up and shook. I must have dropped them inside the satchel while carrying other items at the same time to the car. My relief from finding them outside the car was immense."

After listening to Paul's story and sensing the emotion he expressed to me during his time of uncertainty about the actual location of his car keys, I began to remember a time recently when my wallet disappeared.

Trent and I had traveled to Florida, a ten hour's drive south, in two separate cars in order to have flexibility to go in different directions if necessary once we arrived, and also so she would have room to carry some necessary items for our extended trip. We had a great visit; everything had gone smoothly, and after two weeks we were ready to return home.

As our landlord had requested, we left the room keys on the

kitchen table and locked the door to our rental condo on our way out. Before long, we were two hours into our long drive home to North Carolina when I impulsively checked my rear pants pocket for my wallet. It was not there. I searched the center console with no success. Flashing through my mind were memories of where I'd last used it to make either a cash purchase or use a credit card.

All I could think of was, it had either been packed in one of our many suitcases now stored in the trunks of both cars, or I'd left it in the condo two hours south of our present location on the interstate. Being in two separate cars, I called her on my cell phone and asked her to pull off the road behind me, so I could go through the luggage to see if, by chance, I'd left my wallet in one of them.

She did that and sat inside her car, as I proceeded to unload the many suitcases from both cars and spread them out across the gravel in a long line on the shoulder of the road. One after the other, I opened them and desperately went through everything. My panic increased as I thought about the effort which would be required to replace what was inside that wallet. There was a quantity of cash involved, but my real concern was all the other items inside. There were insurance cards, credit cards, personal photos, my driver's license, various phone numbers of friends, and other important information I really did not want to lose.

As I stood up and surveyed the situation, for the first time I noticed how foolish it must appear to everyone else on the interstate, as they passed. They must have questioned, *what the hell is that guy doing? He's got all those suitcases lined up, one after the other, on the edge of the road. All of them are standing wide open with tumbled clothes inside.*

Yep…it was a scene which could have been taken directly out of one of the *Beverly Hillbillies* movies, but I didn't care. Finding that wallet was all that was important.

I realized my brow was covered with sweat from concern and

stress, as I walked over to Trent's car and said, "I've searched everything, and my wallet is no place to be found. We need to return to the condo, because there's a slim chance I left it under one of the beds. During our stay, I used that as a place for safe keeping because there was no secure safe within the room in which to store valuables."

She understood the predicament, so I closed and reloaded all the suitcases, and we found the closest interstate exit to turn around. All the way south, my mind was working continuously trying to remember where I'd last seen that damn wallet. I also began to think about all the phone calls I'd have to make to notify everyone about its loss and then get replacement cards. It wasn't a pleasant time for me.

Upon arrival, we remembered the owner of the condo had told us earlier to just leave the keys inside and lock the door as we left. We couldn't get back into the condo without those keys. A phone call was made to another location, miles away, where the owner agreed to come by and open the door for us. We waited until finally she arrived and opened the door. The keys we'd left were still lying on the kitchen table, exactly where we'd been told to place them.

The first thing I did was to immediately rush to the bedroom in question and search underneath that bed where I'd been keeping the wallet during our stay. To my surprise, my fingers closed around it, releasing a lot of built-up tension and stress. I was thrilled.

Within minutes, we were back on the road and headed north again. There was a long drive still ahead, and we'd lost close to six hours with that necessary detour. When we finally passed the spot where I'd pulled over and searched all the suitcases, nothing but happiness and relief filled my mind. I patted that wallet in my back pocket and vowed to myself to never let something so completely unnerving ever happen again.

Greenlights

Recently I received a strong recommendation for a good book from a long-time friend, Will Franks.

After having read five of my personal memoir books, he said, "You should take some time and read a new memoir by the well-known movie actor, Matthew McConaughey, named *Greenlights*. It reminds me a lot of what you've already written about yourself, as you told stories from your own life. Your writing styles are somewhat similar."

With those flattering words still ringing in my ears, I felt compelled to visit our local Barnes and Noble bookstore that afternoon to locate a copy. To my surprise, they had it in stock, fresh off the press. Not really knowing what to expect, I rushed home and started reading with great interest. Instantly, the book grabbed my attention.

McConaughey started off with a short introduction where he explained the name he'd chosen for his memoir. In short, throughout his life, he'd viewed the different times when special and unexpected positive happenings had taken place to be 'greenlights.' Those indicated he should move forward and take advantage of the opportunities laid out before him. As I read his words, I quickly realized that his insights and way of viewing the world were enlightening.

He talked about his childhood days, growing up, and how he eventually went through the process of becoming a famous movie actor. Every time, along the way, when he'd received a 'good break,' it had been viewed as a 'greenlight,' or an indication he should continue moving forward in a predetermined direction.

One of the interesting things he talked about early on had to do with the fact he'd kept a personal journal for many years. In that journal, he'd regularly documented the ups and downs in his life as they occurred. Many of his emotions had been written down on paper, so in the future he could recall them in great detail. That information later served him well as he began writing his manuscript. He had also written a variety of short poems over the years that were saved in the same notebook. Many of them were included in his completed memoir.

Another interesting aspect of his book was that throughout his life he'd recorded what he called 'bumper stickers.' Sometimes those were only short thoughts with deep meaning, which he'd written down after seeing them in print. At other times, his 'bumper stickers' were worthwhile phrases he'd thought up himself that would serve well as good advice to follow, and he gave the reasons why. All of them were powerful and scattered randomly throughout his other material.

The book contained, as a whole, valuable information on how to live a productive and successful life in spite of occasional failure. It was all artfully told through his eyes and personal experiences.

Because I really enjoy listening to audio discs in my car while driving, I went back to Barnes and Noble to see if they offered a CD tape of his book. Sure enough, it was there and waiting for me. I bought a six-CD, box set and carried it home with the desire to begin listening immediately. To my surprise, the entire book was read on those discs by Matthew McConaughey, and not by someone else.

The good part about that was his voice, and the way he expressed himself. The highs and lows of his life were all told with special emphasis. I felt as if I had been sitting right beside him as he was telling me his life story, sometimes with occasional laughs, and sometimes conveying the feeling he might want to cry. *Cool stuff...believe me.*

If you want my opinion, I think he's a better writer than an actor, or at least equally proficient at both. I began to envy the depth of what he had to say, the way he said it, and how it made me feel afterwards. Every time I had the opportunity to listen for the next week, I walked away thinking about what I'd just heard.

That's the sign of a truly good book. I encourage you to go purchase it, or even better, buy his audio disc series and take time to listen. You'll come away, as I did, with fresh insights about a unique man who has something important to say about life and says it well to an eager listener.

Thank you, Will, for your wonderful suggestion.

Pain is Relative

A couple of years ago, my brother Jim told me a couple of stories that are worth repeating. Before I get into them, let me first give you some background information.

Jim has endured many years of constant pain in his back due to spinal injuries that he sustained early on in life while playing high school football. During the 60s, both of us played aggressively and often crashed head-on into opposing players at full speed. It was viewed as the thing to do and even respected by others. However, the result for him has been a lifetime of pain that has sometimes been almost unbearable. Somehow, I escaped getting seriously injured while playing alongside of Jim and have not experienced his pain and problems.

Over the last twenty years or more, Jim has undergone several operations on the vertebrae of his back to relieve pressure on the nerves branching off to various parts of his body. To date, he's had eight major spine surgeries, which have covered all the areas from the base of his skull down to his pelvis.

Two of those operations involved the center part of his back where vertebrae were fused together. In the process of fusing them, his surgeon added long rods and screws to hold that area completely rigid, resulting in permanent loss of all flexibility. Afterwards, he could no longer twist and flex as he'd been able to do in the past.

Another time, a number of years ago, he had a series of three major operations on the upper part of the vertebrae in his neck. Because of earlier injuries, calcium had begun to build up in-between the vertebrae, and it had put excessive pressure on the nerves. That caused him a lot of pain, and eventually he started having numbness in his arms and hands.

His surgeon advised him to be operated on but warned him of the seriousness of it. A very bad outcome to the neck region might result in Jim becoming a complete quadriplegic, where he would lose all use of his arms and legs. Without much choice, Jim decided to go forward with the recommended surgery.

The first operation, in that series of three, involved an incision to the back of his neck on the right side, in order to gain access to the affected area. Sections of the vertebrae were split vertically to allow additional space for the spinal cord and nerves. Small chips of bone, that had been earlier removed from his pelvis, were inserted to stabilize the vertically split bones.

The second operation was very similar to the first one, but the incision was made to the back of his neck on the left side. Small bone chips from his hip were again added to fill in the space created by the surgeon to relieve pressure on his spinal cord and nerves.

His final surgery in that series of operations was to the frontside of his neck. For this one, the surgeon removed a badly ruptured and bulging disk and replaced it with bone grafts to fuse the area, being careful to protect the trachea, esophagus and carotid arteries.

After each of these operations, Jim refused to take any pain medication.

He told his surgeon, "If I start taking pills and become dependent on drugs to alleviate pain, I fear I'll never be able to stop using them."

When I heard what he'd said, I was astonished at his decision. I knew if I'd gone through something similar, I would be eating those pain pills like candy.

Jim later told me, "Because of all the problems I've had with my back, someday I'll be forced to take pain medicine regularly to survive. I'm in no hurry to reach that point in my life."

Obviously, the conclusion can be reached that Jim has a high tolerance for pain.

Now…on with the story!

Within the last two weeks, Jim underwent more major surgery on his upper neck. This time it involved the vertebrae directly below his skull. He had been dealing with pain for the last five years so severe that he could hardly sleep at night. When his arms and hands again started to go completely numb, he knew something had to be done.

After having an MRI, with its accompanying X-ray, it was discovered that another disk between one of those upper vertebrae had ruptured. The bulging part between the bones was putting pressure on those nerves causing his current problem. It was explained to him that as much as a 90% blockage was occurring. He had no choice but to go through yet another major surgery to correct the problem.

After three hours of intense surgery, he awoke. When his mind was clear, the surgeon entered his room and said, "Your operation was successful. After a full recovery, you should be able to function normally with no nerve pain and no numbness in your extremities. I know you are a busy man, but I warn you to take it easy for a while during the healing process."

Jim had never wanted to stay in the hospital very long after one of those procedures. He requested, "Doc, is there any way I can now go home? I promise to take it easy, keep ice on my neck to hold down the swelling, and do nothing to injure myself."

It was an unusual request, but his surgeon responded, "I'll allow you to do that if you promise to be careful and come back to see me in a week. I need to take more X-rays to see how you are progressing. Can I prescribe some strong pain killers for you? You're gonna need 'em."

"Nope. I plan to avoid using pain medicine, as I've done in the past."

"Are you sure? The pain could get very bad, once the medicine we've given you for the operation begins to wear off."

"I'll be fine. Don't worry about me. Thanks for the great job you've done. I'll be out of here in the next two hours, if it's okay with you."

"Alright. Be sure to be careful and come back in a week."

The next week passed quickly, and Jim drove to see his surgeon. Upon entering his office, the first thing necessary was for him to get another X-ray, so the doctor could see how the healing process was progressing.

That X-ray was taken and transferred to a computer. Jim peered through his doorway's curtain, just in time to observe the surgeon staring at the image, which was now projected on a large screen in the next room. The surgeon was leaning forward to the point he almost had his nose against the screen. His hands went up to his cheeks, and then his fingers moved nervously through his hair.

Something was wrong. Jim was sure of it by the doctor's reactions. The surgeon lifted his phone and called the X-ray technician.

Jim heard, "Would you please take another X-ray of Mr. Hearn's neck from the side. I need that done immediately."

With some concern, Jim was escorted back to the area and another X-ray was taken. It was quickly transferred to the waiting surgeon in the next room by computer. Jim watched nervously until the doctor raised from his chair and walked into the room where Jim was sitting in a chair.

He said, "I don't know what's going on, but you've scared the shit out of me. When I looked at that first X-ray which was taken from the front, I quickly focused on an unusual metal object that appeared to be connected to your neck vertebrae and extended out to one side. It looked like a large safety pin, about three inches in length." He continued, "When I first saw it on the screen, my heart completely stopped beating for a few seconds, and I broke out in a sweat. I'd never seen anything like it. All I could think of was that I'd somehow left something inside you when we closed your incision. I could envision my entire career ending, with a lawsuit so large I'd lose my home, my car, and all my savings. What in the hell do you have in the back of your shirt? I didn't realize the object was behind your neck until the second X-ray was taken."

Taking off his shirt, Jim began to talk as he examined it, "I put on this clean, starched shirt this morning. In a rush to get here, I didn't look at it closely. There's a metal laundry pin still in the back identifying this shirt as mine. Normally, I take those out after the laundry delivers them to me, but this morning I forgot."

"Now that I know what happened, I can see the humor," the doctor said. "It just freaked me out. This is so unusual; I'll have to tell the story and show that X-ray to all my surgeon friends. They'll be quite amused."

"I'm really sorry. I didn't mean to scare you like that. Honestly, I didn't leave it in there on purpose."

"By the way," the doctor began to ask. "How have you been doing without taking any pain medicine? I've been concerned about you. Normally, my patients stay in the hospital for a couple of days after a surgery like yours and roll around constantly complaining about the pain."

"Well, Doc. Pain is relative."

"What do you mean by that?"

At that point, Jim started telling him the main story I want to share with you.

"Let me explain, Doc. I have a friend whose pain tolerance is unbelievable. No matter what he goes through, he seems to feel no pain."

"That sounds extremely unusual. How can it be true?" he asked.

"Let me continue. Recently, he went to the dentist and discovered he had a badly abscessed tooth. The dentist told him he must have a root canal that would involve a fair amount of pain."

The dentist asked him, "Sir, are you having much pain right now?"

"No, I'm not. My pain tolerance has always been very high. As you know…pain is relative," he said.

"Well…I'll be giving you a shot in the jaw that will completely deaden the area, so I can drill down into the tooth, through the damaged nerve, to perform your root canal. You will need to take pain medication afterwards in order to stand it. Is that okay with you?"

"No sir. I don't want you to give me the shot, and I won't be needing any pain medication afterwards."

"Are you sure? I can't believe you want to go through something like this without a shot to deaden the area and then take pain medication for a day or so afterwards."

"Trust me. I'll be fine," he said.

The operation started and the dentist began to drill through the tooth, right into the sensitive area containing all the nerves. He expected at any moment the fellow to jump out of the chair in pain.

Nothing happened. In fact, the patient went to sleep and seemed to be completely relaxed.

Once the root canal was finished, he woke the man and asked with great interest, "Did you feel any pain?"

"No Sir. Pain is relative."

"You've told me that before, but I still can't wrap my mind around the concept. Please explain further."

"Sure. A few years ago, I went hunting with a couple of my buddies. We were near a large, wooded area surrounded by fields of tall grass, and suddenly I began to feel the need to take a dump. I told them to wait on me, that I would just step about fifty feet away and 'do my business' in the tall weeds, then I'd be right back."

The dentist asked, "What does, 'pain is relative,' have to do with what you're telling me?"

"Hang on…I'm getting there. After I walked farther toward the woods, near a heavily grassed area, I dropped my pants, began to squat, and planned to unload a big pile to relieve myself. Just after I bent my knees and dropped to the level I needed, a large metal bear trap snapped shut. The damned thing grabbed both my hanging balls forcefully, I was immediately stunned."

"Oh, my God. What happened next?"

"I jumped up and started running."

"That must have been extremely painful," he said.

"Where I gained my real tolerance for pain was when the thirty feet of chain, attached to that bear trap, finally ran out."

Surrounded by Wildlife and Nature

Our new home backs up to an expansive freshwater lake, located beside a wide fairway, as part of a well-manicured golf course. Given those two features, it's not hard to imagine how beautiful that panoramic view appears when looking off our large two-story rear deck. With a pair of binoculars in hand, many different types of wildlife can be spotted in great detail, sitting and standing no more than two hundred yards away.

For some strange reason, during this last fall and early winter, huge flocks of different birds began gathering around the lake's shoreline and on the branches of a long row of cypress trees nearby. Within an hour of sundown each night, there are groups of large, white, great egrets that suddenly appear in the sky, all traveling from the same northeast direction. Sometimes they come in groups of three, five, and ten, and at other times as many as thirty will appear in one tight flock. It's a sight to behold with the warm evening sun reflecting off their white bodies, as they cruise above us, just before landing. All of them fly directly over our house on their downward descent to ultimately gather in the branches of those trees. When all of them have arrived, just before it gets too dark to see very clearly, it's easy to count as many as three to four hundred. An entire line of trees becomes filled with white spots as they begin roosting for the night.

The great egret is the largest of the white birds with long, black legs and a straight, yellowish bill used to catch small fish. When I say, 'largest of the white birds,' I'm talking about the smaller, common ones being the snowy egrets and the ibis that are about half the size, but I'm not including the very large mute swans, which we find on the lakes of this area in pairs.

Each morning, around seven o'clock, the same great egrets all leave the trees and fly back over our house in the opposite direction from where they arrived the evening before. I've never seen anything quite like it.

Occasionally, on an overcast morning, many of them remain where they spent the night, with a few landing on the ground close together, where they surround a portion of the shoreline. On those mornings, there may be up to one hundred and fifty spaced out along the bank on both sides of the lake, while some remain perched in the trees.

Just when I thought the gathering of great egrets was one of the more unusual things I'd seen, I counted as many as one hundred great blue herons that decided to take up residency for a day around the same lake. That was truly unique because I've hardly ever observed those large birds gathering with more than two at a time in a specific area. They're normally very solitary wildlife that keep a reasonable distance between themselves and others of the same species.

In light of all that, a few weeks ago I noticed a pair of mute swans that seemed to be taking up residency on the same body of water behind us, allowing them to be viewed daily. Those large white birds can stretch their necks to the point where they appear to be almost four feet tall when standing. At other times, they swim quietly across the surface of the lake and appear quite elegant, while sporting a large body.

On other mornings, I've observed a few hundred large cormorants gather in another set of trees directly across the lake from us. They're unusual birds in that they have light blue eyes and constantly dive for food over and over when swimming around the surface of a lake. I've never seen as many at one time as seemed to gather lately in this area.

So far, I've not seen groups of medium sized, white ibis, with their distinctive downward curved, four-inch-long bills, hanging around this particular spot. Thousands of them are known to roost on a special body of land, full of trees, near Bald Head Island south of here and fly back and forth to this part of Wilmington to feed in grassy fields for the day. That small island on which they roost is known to be one of the largest gatherings for the ibis in North America and located less than twenty miles away. I've heard that up to 12,000 pairs roost on that one island. In past years, I've seen groups of them hanging out in the shallow waters of a nearby lake for a few hours before the late evening, when afterwards they return home.

In addition, there are now migrating ducks of varying species that travel up and down the Eastern Coastal Flyway in groups which gather for a few days at a time on this same lake behind us, before again taking flight to continue on their migration route. I've seen hooded mergansers, redheads, blue wing teals, green wing teals, wood ducks, and of course the common mallards.

There are plenty of Canada geese that feed in a vacant, grassy lot next door where they leave piles of droppings that will easily stick to the bottom of your shoes, to be later tracked into the house. Every spring there are many babies hatched by them to increase their numbers. After they take flight, it's interesting to see them in 'V' shaped formations cruising through the air and making a soft honking noise.

On top of that, recently we've had a four-foot alligator show up on the same lake. He's too small to bother anyone or their pets, but something special to observe as he slowly moves from one location to the other. I'm sure he is currently eating small fish, frogs, and turtles to survive.

That brings to mind the fact our lake is full of turtles. During this past spring, many of the females left there, crossed the golf course fairway, and walked to the vacant lot beside us to dig holes and lay their eggs. We observed many of them do that and then return to the lake. Months later, broken eggshells were noticed laying around in the grass where those babies had hatched and returned to the same body of water. How they know to go in the correct direction to reach the lake is a mystery to me. Somehow, nature takes care of them.

In the extreme eastern edge of North Carolina, in addition to the normal, small grey squirrel, we have an unusually large quantity of fox squirrels. Those animals are at least fifty percent larger in body size than the grey squirrel. There are two distinct species, a silver one and a black one. What's interesting about them is that both versions have white faces, white paws, and white on the ends of their tails. Otherwise, they're either silver or black. The black ones resemble a small skunk when you see them scurrying across the yard from one tree to the other. While growing up in central Tennessee, it was not uncommon for me to occasionally sight a red fox squirrel that was similar in size, but never either silver or black in color. There's a pair of silver ones which live in a big poplar tree just across the road in front of our house. One of them we've named Louie and the other one we refer to as Louise. They're friendly enough and regularly viewed as pets.

Whenever I have the chance to go outside during the night, which occurs more frequently than I prefer, due to my little dog needing to go pee around 1:00, an owl can be heard in a nearby tree. We have both horned owls and barred owls. The horned owl is larger with yellow/orange eyes and the barred owls are a little smaller with solid brown eyes. I've seen both of them perched in trees over the past twenty years.

Ospreys, the same bird as a seahawk, are often seen during the day as they swoop down and catch small fish in lakes around the golf course. They have a characteristic call that can be heard from a long distance, making anyone close by aware they're in the area. If you watch them circle long enough, you'll usually get to see them dive and catch fish using their sharp talons. Those fish are then taken back to a large stick-filled nest in the top of a dead pine tree. Their nests are almost as large as an eagle's nest, if used multiple years in a row.

Only a couple of months ago, I observed a mature American bald eagle flying over that same lake behind us. Its wings were broad, and the head and tail feathers were bright white in color surrounded by a dark brown body. I learned a few years ago that the bald eagle doesn't get those white accents until it's fully mature at around five years of age. When seen, they make a lasting impression.

There seems to always be a large red-tailed hawk or two circling the skies in this area. They're on the watch for small bunny rabbits racing from one clump of grass to the other, isolated field mice, or an unsuspecting grey squirrel that can be easily picked from the side of a big tree. A few years ago, we had a nest of red-tailed hawks in the top of a large tree next to us where three babies were raised. It was very interesting to see them mature and finally fly away when they were about the same size as their parents.

As you can gather from my descriptions, I love wildfowl and wildlife in general. That's why many of my bronze and highly detailed wood sculptures have centered around those types of creatures. It's been fun to spend parts of my time over the last thirty-five years learning about various species. Only by close observation and intense study have I been able to recreate some of the realistic pieces I've worked on, spending hundreds of hours to finish each sculpture.

About the Author

Ed Hearn was born in Nashville, Tennessee on June 26, 1949, and lived in that same general area for his first fifty years. After graduation from Tennessee Technological University, with a Bachelor of Science degree in Business Management, he moved to Hendersonville, Tennessee and worked for thirty years in Nashville at a manufacturing/printing business, where he served as a part-owner.

He has two sons, John and Matt, and two grandchildren, Owen and Isabella. The decision to retire came for Ed well over two decades ago, and he currently lives in the Landfall community located in Wilmington, North Carolina.

Ed enjoys golf, tennis, boating, fishing, traveling, writing, creating highly detailed three-dimensional sculptures made of both wood and bronze, and producing acrylic paintings. Up until 2019, for a period of ten years, he participated in both U. S. National and World Level Masters track and field championships held throughout the United States and many foreign countries around the globe. His specialties were the javelin throw, shot put, and discus events. After winning the coveted World Championship gold medal in the javelin throw, within his five-year age bracket during 2017 in South Korea, he finally decided two years later to retire from his intensive involvement with those aggressive physical activities.

He's been writing his entertaining and thoughtful short stories for the past ten years in an effort to share his colorful life and varied experiences with both his extended family and other interested individuals.

The motivation for him to write and express his feelings in

the form of short stories was the result of him telling both personal and truthful tales during numerous family get-togethers. Those were repeated many times through the years to everyone's enjoyment. He didn't want them to be lost to future generations and finally decided to sit down and create an extensive collection of his often humorous, sometimes self-reflective, and interesting memories.

Ed's previous memoir books, each filled with a large collection of short stories, form a continuous series. Their titles are *Memories of My Journey...Stories from My Youth, Experiences Along My Journey...Stories from a Life Well-Lived, Reflections from My Journey...Stories Worth Repeating, Travels While on My Journey...Major Trips from My Life, and Moments Within My Journey...Stories to be Shared.* Now...his sixth memoir book, in that growing series, is titled, *Additional Stories from My Journey...Staying the Course.*

In addition, Ed has also published three additional novels that were written while working with his younger brother Jim and his younger sister Gail. Those are titled *The Shoeshine Guy, White Beans and Cornbread...Growing Up in the South, and Camo Man.* His fourth novel, written by himself, is titled *Saturdays with Billy Bob...Stories from Grandma's Porch.* He's currently working on two additional books, which will be published in the near future.

There's also a large assortment of his short stories included in each of five separate books written as a collaborative effort and published by the Landfall Writers' Group, of which he's been an active member for over eight years. The titles of those books are *Pieces of Life, Reflections of Life, Memories of Life, Threads of Life, and Moments of Life.*

All of his books are available from Amazon Books in paperback, hardback, or eBook for ease of reading on Kindle or other electronic devices. Each of those are listed on his "Ed Hearn webpage" at: https://www.amazon.com/Ed-Hearn/e/B07MLTZFHX

Made in the USA
Columbia, SC
24 November 2024

47042027R00136